IØ128616

Dreams and Dream Interpretation

Combining the latest neurological research and up-to-date psychoanalytic theory, *Dreams and Dream Interpretation: A Contemporary Introduction* gives readers a clear understanding of dreams, dream work and the ever-changing interpretations of this extraordinary phenomenon.

In this book, Christian Roesler brings together an overview of the development of different theories of dreaming and dream interpretation throughout the history of psychoanalysis, from Freud's seminal papers to contemporary approaches. He provides a thorough outline of empirical dream research and shows the reader how they can be integrated in both therapeutic and theoretical work. Throughout, he illustrates his ideas with solid case studies from his own work. Providing a comprehensive yet impartial perspective on the different theories of dream interpretation, the function of dreams and their use as a tool to mine the depths of the unconscious, this book is a vital step in the development of psychoanalytic dream work.

Part of the *Routledge Introductions to Contemporary Psychoanalysis* series, this book is a vital resource for psychoanalysts, psychologists and psychodynamic psychotherapists, as well as those undertaking psychotherapeutic training. Students and scholars of psychology, psychiatry, anthropology and medicine will gain a thorough understanding of dreams and the inner psyche.

Christian Roesler, Ph.D., is a Professor of Clinical Psychology at the Catholic University of Applied Sciences in Freiburg, Germany, Professor of Analytical Psychology at the University of Basel, Switzerland and Associate Professor of Psychotherapy Sciences at Sigmund Freud University Linz, Austria. He is a Jungian psychoanalyst in private practice in Freiburg.

Routledge Introductions to Contemporary Psychoanalysis

Series Editor: Aner Govrin
Executive Editor: Yael Peri Herzovich

This comprehensive series illuminates the intricate landscape of psychoanalytic theory and practice. In this collection of concise yet illuminating volumes, we delve into the influential figures, groundbreaking concepts, and transformative theories that shape the contemporary psychoanalytic landscape. At the heart of each volume lies a commitment to clarity, accessibility, and depth. Our expert authors, renowned scholars and practitioners in their respective fields, guide readers through the complexities of psychoanalytic thought with precision and enthusiasm. Whether you are a seasoned psychoanalyst, a student eager to explore the field, or a curious reader seeking insight into the human psyche, our series offers a wealth of knowledge and insight.

James F. Masterson: A Contemporary Introduction
Loray Daws

Antonino Ferro: A Contemporary Introduction
Robert Snell

Transgenerational Trauma: A Contemporary Introduction
Jill Salberg and Sue Grand

Schizophrenia: A Contemporary Introduction
Gillian Steggles

Erotic Transferences: A Contemporary Introduction
Andrea Celenza

For more information about this series, please visit: www.routledge.com/Routledge-Introductions-to-Contemporary-Psychoanalysis/book-series/ICP

Dreams and Dream Interpretation

A Contemporary Introduction

Christian Roesler

Routledge
Taylor & Francis Group
LONDON AND NEW YORK

Designed cover image: Designed cover image: © Michal Heiman,
Asylum 1855–2020, The Sleeper (video, psychoanalytic sofa and
Plate 34), exhibition view, Herzliya Museum of Contemporary
Art, 2017

First published 2025
by Routledge
4 Park Square, Milton Park, Abingdon, Oxon OX14 4RN

and by Routledge
605 Third Avenue, New York, NY 10158

*Routledge is an imprint of the Taylor & Francis Group, an informa
business*

© 2025 Christian Roesler

The right of Christian Roesler to be identified as author of this
work has been asserted in accordance with sections 77 and 78 of
the Copyright, Designs and Patents Act 1988.

All rights reserved. No part of this book may be reprinted or
reproduced or utilised in any form or by any electronic,
mechanical, or other means, now known or hereafter invented,
including photocopying and recording, or in any information
storage or retrieval system, without permission in writing from
the publishers.

Trademark notice: Product or corporate names may be
trademarks or registered trademarks, and are used only for
identification and explanation without intent to infringe.

British Library Cataloguing-in-Publication Data
A catalogue record for this book is available from the British
Library

ISBN: 978-1-032-79455-6 (hbk)
ISBN: 978-1-032-74429-2 (pbk)
ISBN: 978-1-003-49207-8 (ebk)

DOI: 10.4324/9781003492078

Typeset in Times New Roman
by Taylor & Francis Books

Contents

Series Editor's Preface

Aner Govrin

Routledge Introductions to Contemporary Psychoanalysis is one of the most prominent psychoanalytic publishing ventures of our day. The series' aim is to become an encyclopedia of psychoanalysis, with each entry given its own book.

Each volume serves as a gateway into a specific aspect of psychoanalytic theory and practice. From the pioneering works of Sigmund Freud to the innovative contributions of modern theorists such as Antonino Ferro and Michal Eigen, our series covers a diverse range of topics, including seminal figures, key concepts, and emerging trends. Whether you are interested in classical psychoanalysis, object relations theory, or the intersection of neuroscience and psychoanalysis, you will find a wealth of resources within our collection.

One of the hallmarks of our series is its interdisciplinary approach. While rooted in psychoanalytic theory, our volumes draw upon insights from psychology, philosophy, sociology, and other disciplines to offer a holistic understanding of the human mind and its complexities.

Each volume in the series is crafted with the reader in mind, balancing scholarly rigor with engaging prose. Whether you are embarking on your journey into psychoanalysis or seeking to deepen your understanding of specific topics, our series provides a clear and comprehensive roadmap.

Moreover, our series is committed to fostering dialogue and debate within the psychoanalytic community. Each volume invites readers to critically engage with the material, encouraging reflection, discussion, and further exploration.

We invite you to join us on this journey of discovery as we explore the ever-evolving landscape of psychoanalysis.

Aner Govrin

Introduction

Ever since Freud's epochal work *The Interpretation of Dreams* (1900), interpreting or working with dreams has had a central status in psychoanalysis. The theories of the dream and its significance, though, as well as the use of dreams in therapy, have changed over time, as well as within various psychoanalytic schools. Furthermore, since the discovery of REM sleep a substantial body of knowledge has arisen, as it has in clinical dream research; this knowledge may contribute to a better evaluation of various theories of the dream in psychoanalysis. It appears to me that these often very interesting research findings, in particular from empirical dream research, are still being widely ignored in psychoanalysis, although they can provide interesting aspects to an understanding of dreams and their application in psychotherapy as well as in psychoanalytic theories. The book seeks to bring together the main themes discussed in relation to dreams in psychoanalysis since Freud with empirical research findings in order to contribute to a further development of psychoanalytic dream theories. Various conceptions of dreams and their significance, as well as their clinical application in psychoanalysis, are reported, with particular reference to the following questions that have determined the debate in psychoanalysis since Freud's time as well as issues in empirical dream research: What exactly is the function of dreaming? Does the dream protect sleep, or does it generate solutions for psychic problems of waking life? Is there a difference between latent and manifest dream content, i.e. does the dream distort the actual unconscious contents, or does it discover them? To that extent, is the dream an encryption of unconscious contents or a

DOI: 10.4324/9781003492078-1

comprehensive self-portrayal of the unconscious? Should the dream be considered as a wish-fulfillment, or does it compensate the conscious mindset? Are the dreamer's associations necessary, or does the dream itself not already provide psychological information about the dreamer? Indeed, does the dream have any meaning at all, as psychoanalysis supposes, or is it a form of meaningless neutral gear of the brain? How is the dream to be worked on in therapy? Must the dream be interpreted / made conscious, or does dreaming in itself, even without being made conscious, have a positive effect on the organism? In this way, an overview of the development of different theories of dreaming and dream interpretation in the history of psychoanalysis is provided. Various theoretical positions on dreams and dream interpretation in the psychoanalytic literature are reviewed (while not providing an exhaustive account, for more details see Vinocur Fischbein, 2011; Jiménez, 2012), with a particular focus on the comparison between Freud's and Jung's conception of dreams, as these two contrast particularly with regard to the questions listed above.

This is followed by an overview of empirical dream research and its findings as far as they are relevant for therapeutic dream work as well as by an overview of clinical dream research, which will be exemplified by research findings and exemplary cases from the author's research.

Various scientific fields have dealt with the phenomenon of dreams: Psychoanalysis, psychotherapy, psychology, consciousness studies, neurosciences, social sciences and humanities, art and cultural studies. The views are quite controversial, and there is no generally accepted definition of dreaming (Windt, 2015). Three deliberately very different explanations are mentioned here as examples.

For Freud, dreams are a disturbing remnant of psychic activity from waking life and

> a special form of our thinking that is made possible by the conditions of the sleep state. It is the dream work that produces this form, and it alone is the essence of the dream, the explanation of its peculiarity.
>
> (Freud, 1900, p. 510f.; emphasis in original)

For the British psychoanalyst Bion (1962; see also Berner, 2018), dreaming is a process that takes place during sleep and also in the waking state (consciousness and the unconscious function simultaneously), is identical to unconscious (waking) thinking and is the prerequisite for the functioning of the psyche. As the basis of all psychological work, the dream ensures the transformation of sensory and emotional perceptions into experience and enables conscious memory, thought and learning processes and thus personality development (Angeloch, 2020). For the neuropsychoanalyst Solms (2011, p. 540), dreaming is

(1) a state of consciousness, characterized by (2) reduced constraints and controls on (3) memory and perceptual imagery with (4) motivational incentive and emotional salience. The occurrence of this hallucinatory mental state during normal sleep probably requires no further explanation than that motivated behavior is precluded during sleep.

In contrast, the definition of a contemporary dream researcher sounds almost simple: Dreaming is simply mental activity during sleep (Schredl, 2018).

On the other hand, empirical dream research has produced an extensive body of knowledge about how dreaming works and how it relates to waking life. These findings have also been incorporated into the development of theories of consciousness and the philosophy of mind and have led to very exciting concepts regarding the functioning of the human mind in general (Windt, 2015).

Before presenting the dream theories and research results, however, it is necessary to discuss the fundamental differences in the interest and in the methods of gaining knowledge in psychoanalysis and in psychotherapy in general on the one hand and in empirical research on the other. Psychoanalysis develops its theories about dreams and their meaning with the aim of using the client's dreams in the context of psychotherapy to make the unconscious conscious; in this sense, the dream is the royal road to the unconscious. The meaning of the dream is (re-)constructed in a dialogical and hermeneutic process in the relationship between analyst and client. The result is therefore always (inter-)subjective meaning with the aim of promoting therapeutic change, and not the discovery of a universally valid or objective meaning of the dream, if this should be possible at all. Clinical dream research, at least insofar as it takes place within psychoanalysis, aims to empirically trace these processes of intersubjective meaning production and their effects on therapy.

Empirical dream research, on the other hand, with its nomothetic claim, aims at generally valid and objective findings about the laws of dreams and their function for the human organism. It is therefore not interested in the subjective meaning of dreams for the dreamer. In addition, in its basic theoretical model, psychoanalysis assumes the mechanisms of a dynamic unconscious in the development of the dream, which implies that the dream also contains meanings that the dreamer cannot and does not want to know. Working with dreams aims precisely to make unconscious content accessible in this sense. For this reason, verifying the correctness of the interpretation – if one can speak of such a thing at all – is epistemologically at least complex, if not problematic. Since the actual core of the dream's meaning is unconscious to the dreamer, he cannot confirm it. From the point of view of psychoanalysis, confirmation is more likely to occur through emotional involvement, the emergence of new material in the therapy session or in further dreams and, in particular, through therapeutic change. This dialectic of finding meaning is not only alien to nomothetically oriented dream research but is explicitly rejected by it. Interestingly, empirical dream research initially set out with the aim of proving that the psychoanalytical view of dreams as having any meaning at all could be refuted. In this respect, it is all the more astonishing that the results of this very research have now confirmed or at least supported many of the original psychoanalytic assumptions about dreams. I therefore regard these results as particularly interesting for psychoanalysis, and it is the aim of this book to present them. In a sense, one could even say that psychoanalysis has ultimately won a victory with its assumptions over the initial aims of empirical dream research. On the other hand, psychoanalysis also makes statements with a claim to general validity, e.g. what the function of dreaming is for the organism, and these can certainly be verified on the basis of empirical research. In my opinion, psychoanalysis in general has so far shied away from engaging with empirical dream research, which is a shame because very interesting results have actually been produced here which also allow various psychoanalytical dream theories to be tested. I think it is very important that psychoanalysis does not surround its theoretical concepts with a wall of immunization strategies, since these concepts, even if they are ultimately intended to serve the intersubjective search for meaning in the context of psychotherapy, certainly have claims to validity of a nomothetic character – and this implies that they must also be subjected to scrutiny. This book aims to contribute to this.

Chapter 1

Dreams and dream interpretation in human history

The phenomenon of dreaming is known to practically everyone, even if some people can remember their dreams better, others less or hardly at all. Dreams and their meaning have always preoccupied people, and even today they often seem strangely meaningful (Barrett & McNamara, 2007). Among the oldest surviving writings of mankind are instructions on dream interpretation or regular dream interpretation books, e.g. the Beatty Papyrus (Egypt around 1800 BC) or the dream interpretation book of Artemidorus of Daldis, ca. 500 BC. In the Gilgamesh Epic (ca. 1200 BC), one of the oldest recorded histories of mankind, a dream and its meaning is also central and determines the further fate of the hero. Bulkeley (2007, 2008) even argues that religions are inconceivable without dreams and their interpretation in a central position. Religion takes its starting point from the phenomenon of the dream, which is understood as a communication from divine or otherworldly powers, and its interpretation.

In the oldest approaches, the original view of the meaning of dreams was that they represented messages from the gods to princes and gave indications of the future. In ancient Greece and also in the Hebrew Talmud, the idea that dreams contain repressed emotions and are related to the dreamer's current life circumstances first emerged (Kramer & Glucksman, 2015). This is also emphasized in the Quran (Bulkeley, 2008): There would be no universally fitting dream interpretations, one would have to put the content of the dream in relation to the dreamer's personality and life circumstances. Even the Sumerians and the ancient

DOI: 10.4324/9781003492078-2

physician Hippocrates assumed that dreams contain important information that can be used to diagnose medical problems. In ancient Greece, there was a tradition of dream incubation. When seeking medical advice and treatment for health problems, people spent a night in the temple of the god of healing, Asclepius, where they slept and dreamed, and the next morning they told the temple priests their dream, from which they then drew clues for diagnosing and treating the illness (Bulkeley, 2008). Fascinatingly, this tradition of dream incubation lives on in some places to this day; for example, on the Greek island of Naxos and in other centers of Orthodox Christianity, such as in Thebes or Bulgaria, where patients sleep in churches while paying attention to their dreams. The Quran also describes a practice called Istikhara, which consists of prayers and certain practices performed before sleep to encourage or induce insightful dreams (Bulkeley, 2008). This practice also continues in modern Islamic countries. For example, popular magazines in Iran offer columns in which readers can send in strange dreams, which are then provided with brief interpretations and practical advice by Muslim psychiatrists.

In modern Europe, on the other hand, it was first questioned whether dreams contained any meaning at all, and it was assumed that they were more a kind of idle brain activity. This view became widespread in the 19th century, and the corresponding scientific debate only really took a new turn with Freud's publication *The Interpretation of Dreams* in 1900.

In contemporary theories of dreams, it is widely accepted that dreams carry meanings and that these are closely linked to the dreamer's waking life and that dream interpretation is a helpful and effective method of psychotherapeutic intervention (Hill, 1996). DeCicco, Donati and Pini (2012) provide an up-to-date overview of studies investigating the effectiveness of therapeutic work with dreams in the context of psychotherapy. They also highlight different therapeutic methods of dream interpretation, including their own Storytelling Method of Dream Interpretation as an example of a more recently developed method.

Psychoanalysis began, in a sense, with dream interpretation (Freud, 1900), and therapeutic work with dreams is still regarded in psychoanalytic schools as the royal road to the unconscious (Fosshage, 1987; Fonagy et al., 2012).

Chapter 2

The dream in Freud

It is important to realize that Freud published his *Interpretation of Dreams* (1900) at a time when, in the course of the Enlightenment, there was a broad consensus in European intellectual history that dreams are not meaningful, that they come about by chance and are something like idle brain activity as opposed to what was assumed in antiquity and the Middle Ages, i.e. that they are messages from God/the gods to the dreamer. Against this background, Freud deserves credit for not only rehabilitating dreams as meaningful but also for creating a coherent scientific theory of how dreams come about, what function they perform for the dreamer and for developing a systematic clinical methodology of how dreams can be interpreted in the context of psychotherapy.

For Freud (1933), the dream basically fulfills a dual function:

> On the one hand, it is ego-appropriate in that it serves the desire to sleep by eliminating the sleep-disturbing stimuli, and on the other hand, it allows a repressed drive to be satisfied under these conditions in the form of a hallucinated wish fulfilment.
>
> (p. 19)

Since repressed urges that arise in sleep could disturb sleep because they are threatening to the ego, they are transformed into the no longer threatening manifest dream content in the course of censorship through dream work (condensation, displacement, visualization, symbolization). These mechanisms of dream work function according to primary process. In this way, "the dream is

DOI: 10.4324/9781003492078-3

the guardian of sleep" (Freud, 1913, p. 398). The dream is a wish fulfillment, it tries to eliminate the sleep disturbance through a hallucinatory wish satisfaction. Freud assumes that the corresponding wishes are stimulated by events that occur during the day, but he only considers such events to be strong enough to produce a dream if they simultaneously awaken unconscious wishes or unsatisfied needs or are linked to them. According to Freud, these are above all the wishes and impulses that emerge from the id. The triggering daily events are then referred to as day residue. Since, according to this understanding, dreams contain the deep unconscious wishes and impulses – albeit in a distorted form – dream interpretation is described as the royal road to the unconscious.

Primary process and dream work

Freud assumes that the human psyche contains two distinct processes: The primary process and the secondary process. The primary process comprises the unconscious processes of our mental life. In dreams, it produces the content of experiences and draws on unconscious wishes. In waking life, this is inhibited by the secondary process. Freud understands the secondary process to be the processes that mediate between the preconscious and the conscious mind. According to Freud, this also includes the ego functions, i.e. cognition, attention, controlled actions and judgment. As the secondary process is reduced during sleep, the primary process is correspondingly less inhibited. Therefore, in dreams, wishes can rise from the unconscious into the conscious mind via the primary process. These then become hallucinatory and visible as dreams. However, as these wishes are too frightening for the conscious mind and could wake the dreamer, they must be made unrecognizable by the secondary process. The secondary process functions in the dream like a censor that disguises the original dream content in order to protect sleep.

Freud uses the term dream work to summarize the various mechanisms that are used in dreams to make the unconscious wishes unrecognizable. These mechanisms include condensation (the condensation of different ideas and images into one), displacement (a potentially frightening image is replaced by a similar but less frightening image), visualization (thoughts are translated into visual content) and symbolization (a neutral object represents a sexual one or one that is associated with it). Through these four mechanisms, the rising desires, together with the rest of the day and childhood memories, are condensed into a dream.

For the methodology of dream interpretation, this means that starting from the manifest dream content, the path back to the latent dream content must be found. In his *Introductory Lectures on Psycho-Analysis* (Freud, 1916, p. 112), he sets out three rules for this:

1   One does not concern oneself with what the dream seems to say, be it complete or absurd, clear or confused, since it is in no way the unconscious we are looking for [...]
2   one limits one's work to awakening the substitute idea for each element, does not think about them, does not check whether they contain anything suitable, does not care how far they lead away from the dream element;
3   wait until the hidden, sought-after unconscious arises of its own accord, [...]

Freud emphasizes that only through the associations of the drea- mer is it possible to return from this manifest surface content of the dream to the actual latent dream content.

Freud's method of dream interpretation using the example of the "dream of Irma's injection"

Freud exemplifies his method at a central point in *The Inter- pretation of Dreams* using an example of a dream that has since gained historical significance in the history of psychoanalysis. In the introduction, Freud discusses the problem that he could not simply publish and analyze his patients' dreams in a publication due to confidentiality, which is why he takes the step of subjecting one of his own dreams to his dream interpretation method. This "dream of Irma's injection" was dated July 24, 1895, and he himself considered this interpretation to be particularly successful.

The dream refers to a patient of Freud's who was also a close friend of the family. Irma, her code name, had originally approached Freud about her hysterical anxiety. The analysis had been partially successful up to this point; the main symptoms had disappeared, but certain physical symptoms persisted. Freud suggested a solution, rather atypical of the analytic approach, but this was not an option for Irma. The treatment was interrupted during her vacation. A doctor friend of Freud's meets the patient on vacation and learns that she is better but not really well, which he reports to Freud. This makes Freud unhappy, but he puts aside the feelings associated with it. The evening before the dream, he tries to write down the previous anamnesis and the course of the therapy in order to pass it on to a colleague. Freud then dreams the aforementioned dream:

A large hall – many guests we are receiving. – Among them Irma, whom I immediately take aside to answer her letter, as it were, to reproach her for not yet accepting the solution. I tell her: If you're still in pain, it's really only your fault. – She replies: If you only knew how much pain I have now in my throat, stomach and body, it makes me cringe. – I am startled and look at her. She looks pale and haggard; I think I'm missing something organic after all. I take her to the window and look down her throat. She shows a bit of bristling, like the women who wear false teeth. I think to myself that she doesn't need it. – The mouth then opens well, and I find a large white spot on the right, and elsewhere I see extensive white-grey scabs on the strange curly formations, which are obviously modelled on the nasal conchae – I quickly call in Dr. M., who repeats and confirms the examination … Dr. M. looks quite different from usual; he is very pale, limps, is beardless on the chin … My friend Otto is now also standing next to her, and friend Leopold examines her over the bodice and says: She has an attenuation on the lower left, also points to an infiltrated area of skin on the left shoulder (which I can feel like him despite the dress) … M. says: No doubt, it is an infection, but it doesn't matter; there will be dysentery and the poison will be excreted … we also know immediately where the infection comes from. Friend Otto recently gave her an injection with a propyl preparation, propylene ... propionic acid ... trimethylamine (whose formula I see printed in bold) ... one does not make such injections so lightly ... probably the syringe was not clean either.

(1900, p. 112)

Freud now subjects this dream to his own method by collecting his own associations to the individual sections of the dream text. It becomes clear that at the center of the events is the patient's unsatisfactory treatment and how this can be explained or who is to blame: First, Freud blames the patient herself for not accepting the solution; moreover, he is not responsible for the physical side of her illness. The other participants also make accusations: Infection is a ridiculous diagnosis, the injected preparation is pointless and the syringe is contaminated. In this collection of associations, Freud as the dreamer realizes that his central concern is that he should not be blamed. This leads him to his central thesis: "The dream represents a certain state of affairs as I would like to see it; its content is therefore a wish fulfillment, its motive a wish" (Freud, 1900, p. 123). The central wish in the case presented here is, according to Freud himself: "concern for health, one's own and others', medical conscientiousness" (p. 125).

The mechanisms of dream work

When collecting his associations to the dream, Freud notices that the relatively straightforward dream text conceals a whole wealth of connections to memories, experiences, relationships, repressed material etc., which are brought together in a relatively small space in the dream, which Freud refers to as **condensation**. This means that several strands of experiences, memories etc. may be summarized in one element of the dream, which can only be differentiated again through the associations. Another process characteristic that Freud describes in his analysis of the dream is called **displacement**. This means that certain elements of the true wish or dream thought contained in the dream are replaced by other elements from the dreamer's waking life. The dreamer is supposed to be distracted from the actual but threatening dream content and come up with other thoughts; the thematic focus is shifted, so to speak.

Freud's general idea is that dreaming does a piece of work for the psyche, the so-called dream work, whereby the potentially dangerous content for the consciousness, the unconscious dream thoughts, are transformed into something else that does not threaten the consciousness. The result of this dream work is the manifest dream content, i.e. the dream as we experience it. The underlying unconscious dream thoughts and unconscious wishes – which, because they have been warded off, should not come into consciousness – represent the latent dream content. The dream work transforms the latent into the manifest content and in this way serves to protect the ego in sleep because otherwise it would be startled by the confrontation with the undisguised content and then wake up. Therefore, "the dream is the guardian of sleep" (Freud, 1900, p. 239). The aim of dream interpretation is to reverse these processes of dream work, i.e. the transformation of the actual latent content into the manifest content, in order to make the unconscious thoughts and wishes accessible in this way.

According to Freud, the actual content of the dream is distorted or masked by the dream work. This happens because even censorship in dreams cannot completely eliminate the psychic energy contained in the unconscious wishes, but it can at least transform it into content that appears harmless. Another element of dream work, **symbolization**, also serves this purpose, in which the latent dream thoughts are translated into a pictorial language. In this dream example, this would be Dr. M. with his syringe, which is intended to cover up a possible treatment error on the part of the dreamer, possibly even a sexual desire. The symbol appearing in the dream thus has a distorted function on the one hand because it is supposed to conceal the latent dream content, and on the other hand it has a pictorial or linguistic – i.e. in the broadest sense symbolic – connection with the content it replaces.

This reveals a certain ambiguity or inconsistency in Freud's conception. On the one hand, Freud emphasizes the problem of a one-to-one relationship "between the symbol and the actual thing for which it stands" (Freud, 1900, p. 356). On the other hand, however, elsewhere he lists a whole catalog of such one-to-one settings, so-called secure dream symbols. Freud argues, for example, that there is virtually no symbol that is incapable of representing sexual facts and desires, and then goes on to explain: All elongated objects (sticks, tree trunks, umbrellas, long sharp weapons, nail files, pistols, neckties) stood for the male sexual organ, while boxes, chests, cabinets, chests of drawers, caves, etc. stood for the uterus. Rooms in dreams are usually women, and if you walk through a series of rooms in a dream, it is therefore a brothel or harem. This appears to be a somewhat simplistic equation, and not only from the point of view of contemporary symbol theory.

Finally, Freud also assumes that the dream is reviewed by consciousness shortly before waking and undergoes a so-called **secondary processing**, i.e. a more coherent composition is created from possibly disparate dream elements, which is due to "consideration for comprehensibility" (Freud, 1900, p. 279). Freud summarizes the result:

> Dream thoughts and dream content lie before us like two representations of the same content in two different languages, or rather, the dream content appears to us as a translation of the dream thoughts into another form of expression. The dream content is given, as it were, in a pictorial script, the signs of which are to be translated individually into the language of the dream thoughts. One would obviously be misled if one wanted to read these signs according to their pictorial value instead of according to their sign relationship.
>
> (p. 284)

Problems and further developments

Freud already found it difficult to use this theory to explain the occurrence of post-traumatic nightmares, in which the traumatic event is repeated virtually undistorted in the dream, associated with great fear and suffering for the dreamer, and it is not uncommon for the dreamer to wake up as a result of the dream – the dream is therefore unable to fulfill its function as a guardian of sleep. Despite great theoretical efforts, he ultimately had no choice but to describe the post-traumatic dream as a dark and gloomy subject.

This formulation of Freud's theory largely corresponds to the view expressed in *The Interpretation of Dreams* (1900). However, it should be noted that Freud repeatedly addressed the understanding of the dream in the course of his works and that the theory evolved (for an overview of Freud's theoretical developments, see Vinocur Fischbein, 2011). For example, Binswanger and Wittmann (2019) point out that Freud revised the theory from *The Interpretation of Dreams* in his work *Abriss der Psychoanalyse* (1938) and attempted to harmonize it with the structural model he had developed in the meantime. Although he retains the elements described above, he adds a second level of processing by the conscious ego, in which the confused and potentially frightening content of the latent dream thought is transformed into a plot that makes more sense and thus meets the requirements of the secondary process.

In 1900, Freud still focused on the guardian function for sleep and the fulfillment of unconscious wishes. Over time, this evolved into a way of looking at the dream as a meaningful psychic act that can be treated like a communication; furthermore, the context for understanding the dream narrative became increasingly important (Vinocur Fischbein, 2011). While the dream work encodes the actual unconscious content, the dream as such, in particular through the processes of symbolization, provides the dreamer with access to unconscious content that would otherwise not be possible. At this point, Freud provides the basis for later views that the dream can be regarded as a communication about unconscious content within the therapeutic relationship. The so-called day residue plays a role here: Freud emphasizes that the dreams of the night usually take up events of the previous day, but place them in a different context. He assumes that the day's events activate unconscious wishes and conflicts, which then become the focus of the dream. In this respect, the dream, even if it distorts the content, brings unconscious themes to the surface. Thus, while for Freud the dream was initially important for understanding the defense against unconscious drive desires, in the course of his development the focus shifted to an examination of its significance for the transference relationship.

Towards the end of his life, Freud stated that psychoanalysts had lost interest in dreams and dream interpretation. Even if this is correct, this has changed again since the 1970s at the latest. Since then, there has been a growing interest in dreams but also in empirical research into dreams and dream processes in psychotherapy, whereby this research and newer concepts are also influenced by the progress made in empirical dream research. However, in the Freudian tradition, especially under the influence of Kleinian theory, the dream has lost its status as the "royal road to the unconscious". It has been replaced by the analysis of transference and countertransference. Transference dynamics also play a central role in the interpretation of dreams (Morgenthaler, 1986). In this view, the dream takes on the significance of a communication within the analytic relationship, e.g. a commentary on the transference relationship.

Chapter 3

Controversies in psychoanalysis over (Freud's) dream theory

From the beginning, the psychoanalytic understanding of the dream and the practice of dream interpretation have been controversial in the psychoanalytic community itself. The debate and the development of psychoanalytic dream theories has circled around a few central questions:

1 Dreaming is universal in humans, but what is its function? Does dreaming protect sleep? Is the dream a wish fulfillment? Or does it aim to solve psychological problems and develop the personality? Does it do this by compensating for consciousness?

2 Does the dream distort the actual unconscious content, i.e. is there a coding/censorship in Freud's sense, or does the manifest dream already contain the actual unconscious content? Is the dream in this sense a communication, e.g. in the relationship between analyst and analysand?

3 How should the dream be worked with in psychoanalytic therapy? Do we need the dreamer's associations in order to understand the meaning? Or does the dream itself already contain the information that can be used therapeutically and which at least sheds light on unconscious aspects of the dreamer's personality and dynamics?

4 In order for the dream to have a constructive effect, does it have to be interpreted/made conscious, or does dreaming in itself have a positive effect on the organism, even without becoming conscious?

DOI: 10.4324/9781003492078-4

From the very beginning, Freud's theory of dreams was controversial in psychoanalysis, perhaps even more controversial than
other concepts. Various early psychoanalysts advocated concepts
that were diametrically opposed to Freud's; not only Jung (as
described in detail below), but also Adler, Maeder and others (see
Berner, 2018). Here, for example, is the position of Alfred Adler:

> Dreams are not isolated psychic phenomena. They make use of
> the same mental dynamics as those used in promises, day-
> dreams, fantasies and other waking behavior. [...] The findings
> of individual psychology indicate that a person's entire behavior
> is uniformly oriented and an expression of his or her respective
> lifestyle. Because dreams are a form of human behavior, they
> cannot be an exception. They are part of the unity.
>
> (Adler, 2010, p. 592f.; transl. C.R.)

Hannich (2018), a contemporary follower of Adler's approach,
emphasizes the importance of self-esteem regulation:

> The basic idea of individual psychology in relation to dreams is
> the unity of waking and dream consciousness. In waking and
> sleeping, people are subject to one and the same striving not to
> let their self-esteem sink. Similar to childhood memories,
> dreams are therefore an expression of lifestyle. The dreamer
> only allows what is of typical lifestyle significance for them.
>
> (Hannich, 2018, p. 99)

These statements are interesting in light of the fact that they largely correspond to a very prominent thesis in today's dream
research, the so-called continuity hypothesis of waking and
dreaming (see below).

Encoding or representation/communication?

Perhaps the most extreme oppositional position to Freud was
taken by the American Ego Psychologists, in particular Hartmann, Kris and Erikson, who believed that dreams were, clinically
speaking, a communication like any other and of no particular use

in revealing the unconscious (Berner, 2018). Erikson (1955), for example, used the famous Irma dream to show that much of the general functioning of the personality could already be read from the manifest dream. Another view attributes the dream primarily a communicative function in psychoanalytic treatment: Infantile object relationships are depicted in the dream which also appear in the transference but can be made the subject of conversation via the dream interpretation. The transference dynamic then also plays a central role in the interpretation of the dream (Morgenthaler, 1986). In this view, the dream takes on the significance of a communication within the analytic relationship, e.g. a commentary on the transference relationship.

Some theories treat the dream under the overarching metaphor of the theater, which makes it possible to distinguish between different spaces, e.g. the stage space and the audience space: The ego is seen as a director on the stage who strives to ensure that everything runs smoothly. But the spectators interfere and act as troublemakers.

> In one room, things are presented that are not accepted by the other part. Concepts such as splitting, denial, defense emerge. The dream is understood as a message that gives the dreamer the task of doing integrative work, of listening to this 'inner voice'.
>
> (Moser, 2003, p. 647)

Dream theories of this kind can be found in Self-Psychology and in the Kleinian school (Moser, 2003). Freud had strictly rejected this view: "The dream does not want to tell anyone anything. It is not a vehicle of communication" (Freud, 1916, p. 238).

In her overview of the development of psychoanalytical dream theories, Vinocur Fischbein (2011) summarizes that there is now a clear tendency to see the function of dreams less as an expression of unconscious wishes (Freud) and more as a representation of the state of the (disturbed) inner world. She summarizes her own view as follows: "[...] that dreams reported in session are communicative signs, capable of being transformed into a symbolic matrix that generates processes of psychic semiosis. They are polysemic messages with an intrinsic value not entirely dependent on the analytic dialog" (Vinocur Fischbein, 2011, p. 341).

Wish fulfillment or creative problem solving?

Freud's hypothesis that dreams are wish fulfillment has been the subject of intense criticism within psychoanalysis from the very beginning.

> To this day, the wish theory has many opponents [...] Freud also reaped disappointment when he qualified his view that dreams, if wish fulfillment could not be represented, were at least an attempt at wish fulfillment or unconscious wish fulfillment. However, these wishes can be found through artful analysis. Many dream experts on both sides of psychoanalysis criticize this as an immunization strategy, saying that one can always interpret dreams in such a way that they amount to wishes. That proves nothing. The question of the regulative functions of the regressive sleep state is undecided.
> (Boothe, 2018, p. 61; transl. C.R.)

Morgenthaler (1986) attempted to reconceptualize Freud's wish hypothesis: According to him, the dream influences the psychoanalytic relationship in that it reveals what the analyst and the analysand do not initially want to know or hear, thus providing clues for the further development of the therapy. Among the more recent critics of the wish fulfillment hypothesis, Bollas (1987) does not completely reject this hypothesis, but clearly relativizes it. The dream is no longer seen here as a pure defense against the wish but as a possible source of knowledge, which can be shown by the fact that many people allow the experiences in their dreams to have a clear influence on their real everyday actions.

Revaluation of the manifest dream content

In more recent theories, especially under the influence of ego psychology, there is a clear trend towards the revaluation of the manifest dream content: "It is increasingly assumed that the manifest dream provides information about the state of the analysand and about their possibilities of understanding their own inner world and the inner world of others (admittedly only in fragmented form)" (Moser, 2003, p. 650), and that information can be gained directly from the manifest dream even without associative decoding. In this sense, interpretations of dreams enable access to the dreamer's personal theory of mind, a more recent view of dreams that is particularly emphasized in Fonagy et al. (2012).

Hartmann's (1995, 1998) view of the autotherapeutic function of dreams can be placed in the same line. In post-traumatic nightmares, the real experience is initially relived very realistically and undistorted, which speaks against a distortion or encoding of the dream content. The function of the dream here would therefore not be to distort the actual content, but rather to transform it so that it can be integrated into long-term memory.

Jung's theory of dreams and dream interpretation

As Jung's view on dreams and dream interpretation marks the maximum difference to Freud's position, it will be presented here in more detail. Over the course of his career, Jung set out his view of the significance of dreams and of working with dreams in psychotherapy in several publications. In 1925, Jung described the dream as a "spontaneous self-portrayal of the current situation of the self in symbolic form of expression" in his treatise "General Points of View on the Psychology of Dreams" (Jung, 1971, §505). This already makes clear a central difference to Freud's view: The dream does not contain a coded message hidden behind the text of the dream. It is not distorted by dream censorship, but according to Jung it is exactly what it represents. However, the unconscious, whose spontaneous expression is the dream, uses a pictorial or symbolic language. In order to use the dream message psychologically and make it accessible to the conscious mind, the language of the dream must be translated into a psychological or conceptual language. Part of the view of the dream as a self-representation of the psyche is the so-called interpretation on the subject level. Viewing the dream at the object level corresponds to everyday understanding. This means that if a dream is about a real person or figure, the dream also deals with this real person or the relationship to them. The interpretation on the subject level, on the other hand, understands all figures appearing in the dream as personifications for parts of the dreamer's personality. This opens up a horizon of interpretation in the dream work, through which the dreamer's own previously unconscious parts can be made accessible.

In Jung's view, the dream originates from the Self, the central stance in the psyche, which on the one hand encompasses the totality of all psychic functions and on the other hand drives the person's development towards this potential wholeness. Jung refers to this movement from the Self towards wholeness of the person as the individuation process. Every dream thus represents a potential building block of the individuation process, with which the Self (Jung often uses the term "the unconscious" as a synonym) sends a message to the conscious mind about how it can orient itself towards its own wholeness. According to Jung, dreams therefore also have a prospective function, i.e. they look ahead to what is missing or needs to be integrated in order to realize wholeness. This is contrasted with the reductive function of dreams, in which current events in dreams are traced back to underlying conflicts in the dreamer's personality, which in turn are linked to past experiences – here Jung sees the connections very similarly to Freud. Jung described an exemplary course of an individuation process in a series of dreams in "Individual Dream Symbolism in Relation to Alchemy" in 1944 (Jung, 1972).

Jung generally describes the relationship of the unconscious to consciousness as compensatory, which refers precisely to the corrective attitude of the unconscious, which is oriented towards wholeness:

> The more one-sided and the further away from the optimum of life possibility the conscious attitude is, the more likely it is that vivid dreams of strongly contrasting, but appropriately contrasting content will occur as an expression of the psychological self-control of the individual.
>
> (Jung, 1984, § 286?)

One could also say that the unconscious offers the conscious mind possible solutions to the conflicts in which it finds itself, or at least makes suggestions as to how the problem can be viewed from a broader perspective. In practical dream work, the dream is therefore always considered in terms of what its compensatory aspect is in relation to the current attitude of the conscious mind (Jung, 1944). In Jung's view, the symbols and images in dreams are not distortions of the actual dream content but correspond to the usual language of the unconscious. In order to interpret these, the symbols appearing in the dream are enriched with mythological parallels in a process known as amplification, in order to come closer to their meaning (Roesler, 2021).

Jung thus clearly ascribes a self-healing potential to dreams. Ermann (2005) sums up Jung's view in comparison to Freud's:

> For Freud, the focus is on the function of the dream as the 'guardian of sleep', i.e. the intention of not allowing the repressed to intrude disturbingly into the consciousness of my sleep. For Jung, it is the communication from the unconscious that makes us dream the dream. [...] In short, for Jung dreams reveal, for Freud they conceal the unconscious.
>
> (p. 44; transl. C.R.)

Although Jung himself repeatedly stated that he had no dream theory, two different dream theories can be identified in his work:

1   the dream is a spontaneous self-representation of the situation of the psyche.
2   the dream compensates for the conscious attitude.

In my opinion, both theories can be combined in a common version: Both theories emphasize that through the dream new – and potentially healing – information is brought to the consciousness. After all, the self-presentation theory is also concerned with the fact that self-presentation occurs from the perspective of the unconscious and is therefore more comprehensive than the perspective of the conscious mind. In accordance with Jung's general view, as it emerges from the tenor of his theoretical presentations, the function of the dream could be summarized as follows:

In dreams, new information is made accessible to consciousness. The unconscious as the source of dreams has more comprehensive information than the conscious mind and communicates this to the conscious mind in symbolic form through dreams. The greater the tension between the state of consciousness and the developmental tendency of the unconscious, the stronger the dream will be in terms of correction or even criticism. The dream in its images and symbols does not represent coded information, but means what it is. The dream language is the language of the unconscious, but in order to be understood and used by the conscious mind, it must be translated into a psychological language. For Jung, symbol means that various meanings coincide in the dream image (Greek: symbolein), i.e. they are condensed, so to speak, and thus every interpretation always reflects less than the original information content of the dream. In contrast to Freud, however, for whom the dream conceals the actual unconscious content (censorship), for Jung the dream is the best form of expression for the unconscious content – i.e. the dream reveals the unconscious.

> In every instance the dream presents contents which compensate the attitude of ego consciousness. Thus, dreams are neither seen necessarily as a wish fulfillment, nor are they seen as being distorted, disguised, and governed by a censor. It would follow that the dream is not necessarily the guardian of sleep, and that it may just as often awaken the dreamer.
>
> (Kirsch, 1968, p. 1460)

Jung also assumes that this function of the dream for the personality as a whole leads to the same themes being taken up again and again in dreams over time – unless they are dealt with analytically. Then a further development should become apparent: Repetitive themes disappear and new ones emerge.

It should be noted at this point that Jung was by no means the only early psychoanalyst who, in contrast to Freud's wish fulfillment theory, advocated a compensation theory of dreaming; Adler (1913), Maeder (1913), Schultz-Henke (1949) and Siebenthal (1953) stand in the same line (cited in Deserno, 1999).

A case example

A client seeks psychotherapy, initially because she is unhappy in her marriage. After the birth of their two children, she gave up her job, while her husband works full-time. The couple therefore have a fairly traditional division of roles: She takes care of the household and looks after the children, while he is the breadwinner. This alone makes the client very unhappy. The conflict is sparked by her husband's desire to have a hot meal cooked for him in the evening. The client is repeatedly outraged by this demand in therapy. However, she rejects the therapist's suggestion that she should discuss this problem with her husband – that would not be possible. Against the background of the biographical anamnesis, it becomes clear that this inhibition to deal with the conflict is based on biographical experiences and imprints. The client is the youngest of three siblings, whereby her two brothers were significantly older than her, which meant that she alone experienced herself as rather weak within the family. In addition, a very traditional, not to say patriarchal, concept of gender roles prevailed in her family of origin. The client's mother had no education and had been exclusively a housewife and mother all her life. The two brothers felt encouraged by this latent devaluation of the female role to bully the client, with the client's descriptions suggesting that this was downright abuse. As a child, the client did not receive any protection from her parents. This suggests the psychodynamic consideration that, on the one hand, considerable anger has built up at this oppression by male family members and, on the other hand, an inhibition of aggression and a low self-confidence in her role as a female being, in the sense that she has the image of herself as being unable to counter male demands in a relationship.

The first few months of therapy were rather uniform: The client was angry and indignant about the division of roles in her marriage, but she rejected any suggestion to discuss this in the relationship or to bring in her ideas about partnership. Then one day the client comes to the therapy session very upset and reports the following dream:

I am walking through a beautiful, large house, the rooms are connected by large double doors. I walk through the rooms, which are painted in different colors. I find it very appealing, perhaps there is too little furniture and furnishings, but overall, I like the house. While I'm still walking around, I hear noise from outside, from the street. As I look out of the window, I see an excavator tearing up the road to lay new pipes. While I'm still looking out, the excavator leaves the construction site and heads towards the house. It smashes through the wall into the house at full speed and into the room I'm standing in. I am terribly frightened and wake up.

Against the background of the client's biography and the complex of low self-confidence and inhibition of aggression described above, this dream image can be understood as follows: Since no known persons or elements appear in the dream, the components of the dream are interpreted at the subject level. In this sense, the house can be understood as an image of the client's overall personality. The large, appealing rooms in different colors can be understood here as a psychological health of the overall personality in the broadest sense; different emotions are differentiated and accessible. However, the lack of furnishings may be an expression of the fact that the client has not yet exhausted the possibilities of her personality or has not yet differentiated them; in a sense, she is not yet "living in the house of her personality". The digger in the dream can be understood as an image of constructive aggressiveness. Constructive aggressiveness here means that the person is able to put forward their own needs and interests and to use a certain degree of aggressive assertiveness to do so. An excavator in general is not only used to destroy something but ultimately also to create something new – in this case, to lay new pipes to improve the supply. The fact that the digger breaks into the house with force can be understood as an image of the fact that the client has so far split off or not yet developed the ability to be constructively aggressive in her life and especially in relationships – which is why she experiences this ability as something threatening and potentially destructive. However, this ability wants to be integrated into the "house" of her overall personality. This would be the compensatory aspect of the dream.

The client's dream could therefore be interpreted as follows: The dream wants to make it clear to her that aggressiveness does have a constructive aspect and is capable of creating something new and helpful. She wants to become aware of this ability and make it part of her overall personality, as an ability that she can consciously and willingly dispose of. What is more problematic is her prevailing attitude, which rejects this aspect of herself and regards it as destructive. In this respect, the dream can compensate for or correct her attitude of consciousness.

The client was not very impressed by this interpretation and initially dismissed it as irrelevant. Interestingly, however, she subsequently began to increasingly confront her husband with her anger and dissatisfaction and to actively deal with the conflict with him.

Chapter 4

Recent psychoanalytic dream theories

The controversies mentioned above, together with the general changes in psychoanalytic theories and treatment approaches over the course of the 20th century, impacted the theorizing around dreams and resulted in changes in how therapeutic dream work was conducted. As already mentioned, it is not the intention here to provide a comprehensive overview of the various theories and their developments within psychoanalysis. Vinocur Fischbein (2011) and Jiménez (2012) provide an overview of the development and current status of psychoanalytic dream theories. Some of the most prominent approaches and new theories in this context are described in this chapter.

The work of Bion

A significant change was brought about by the work of Bion (1962, 1967), who regarded the dream as a fundamental psychic function. While for Freud, dream work served to distort the latent dream content in order to protect sleep, following Bion, dreams are understood as a special form of unconscious thinking that serves to process conflicts, create new ideas and promote mental growth. Bion proceeds here from his theory of the "alpha-function": "It seemed convenient to suppose an alpha-function to convert sense data into alpha-elements and thus provide the psyche with the material for dream thoughts …" (1962, p. 182). This constitutes a hypothetical mechanism that transforms sensory perceptions in the raw state (beta-elements) into alpha-elements, i.e.

DOI: 10.4324/9781003492078-5

building blocks of the psyche, which are put to use both in unconscious, symbolic thinking in the waking state and in dreams. By this mechanism, unprocessed primary experience is transformed into something with which the psyche can work, which make thinking, memory storage and remembering and thus mental growth possible. The alpha-elements are used in dreaming to form dream thoughts. The very interesting thought here is that dreamlike processes occur both in the waking and in the sleeping state, which is being accepted in more recent dream theories, especially from the field of consciousness research (see below). Bion thus accords the dream and unconscious thinking a creative capacity for working out conflicts, creating new ideas, and psychic growth. In contrast to Freud's model of dream interpretation, this perspective is no longer concerned with the interpretation of unconscious wishes but with the generation of representations and symbolizations. This approach goes so far as to claim that the dream is not the guardian of sleep, but rather that sleep is the guardian of the dream, i.e. that dream work is important for mental and psychological health and growth and that sleep is a prerequisite for this. Bion also emphasizes that Freud only recognized the defensive function of dreams and overlooked their creative function. Insight does not occur only in the making conscious but also in the process of the dream-thought itself. Meltzer (1983) expressed a similar view: Dreaming is "a creative process which generates meaning that can be deployed to life and relationships in the outside world" (p. 83).

The cognitive information-processing model of Moser and von Zeppelin

Moser and von Zeppelin (1996) have developed a generative model with the addition of information processing models from psychology and neuroscience. It sees dreams as a cognitive and affective information processing mechanism that serves to solve psychological problems. Affect regulation is at the center of the dream model, although it should be noted that it is not an interpretation model but an explanatory model for how dreams are generated.

Essentially, the dream process is about processing traumatic and conflictual emotional experiences by repeatedly attempting to dream, think and integrate previously undigested emotional experiences between the two regulatory contexts of the safety principle and emotional involvement. The dream is understood as a micro-world that represents a problem-seeking structure with the aim of solving problems.

(Döll-Hentschker, 2008, p. 83; transl. C.R.)

Based on this theory, the authors have developed a coding model that can be used to examine the process of dreams in psychotherapy.

Briefly summarized, this model postulates that so-called dream complexes – activated by current events – process all information of unresolved conflicts and traumatic situations during dreaming. The dream searches for a solution or, rather, for the best possible adaptation of these dream complexes [...]. It is postulated that a dream complex originates from one or more such complexes that are stored in long-term memory. These complexes in turn are rooted in conflictual and/or traumatic experiences, which we encounter again in condensed form in the form of introjects. They correspond to Freud's latent dream thoughts. They are activated by external stimuli that are structurally similar to the stored situations of the complexes and urge us to find a solution. The search for a solution to these complexes is determined by the need for security and the desire for participation. [...] Desires play a specific role within these complexes by linking ideas about the self with ideas about others and with generalized representations of interaction (RIGs, i.e. how the self imagines that interaction usually takes place). Conflictual complexes are areas of bundled desires, RIGs and self and object models with repetitive character, characterized by unbound affective information.

(Fischmann et al., 2012, p. 849)

Hartmann's theory of the autotherapeutic function of dreams

On the basis of his study of post-traumatic nightmares, Hartmann (1995, 1998) assumes an autotherapeutic function of dreams. Freud had already dealt with the explanation of nightmares after traumatic experiences, in which the real course of the traumatic event is repeatedly and realistically relived, which was in contrast to his dream theory. Hartmann was now able to observe a process whereby, shortly after the traumatic event, it is relived in the dream, like a movie, and the event appears unchanged in the dream. Some time after the event, however, there are changes in the dream: The place or the people involved are changed. Finally, the real events are partially replaced by symbolic representations. Hartmann assumes that in the dream, in a safe place where no new sensory input takes place, new connections are created and the violent emotionality is thus calmed and integrated. The dream supports integrative processes by contextualizing the emotions. Dreams process irritating experiences that are accompanied by agitated or anxious affects, and in the dream an attempt is made to create links to other experiences in memory in order to incorporate the painful experience into long-term memory with other, less emotionally charged memories.

Control-mastery theory

The most developed theory in this area is certainly the so-called control-mastery theory (Gazzillo, Silberschatz, Fimiani, De Luca & Bush, 2019), which was developed by psychoanalysts from the San Francisco Psychotherapy Research Group and which incorporates many of the results and concepts of empirical dream research presented below:

A dream is an unconscious attempt to find a solution to an emotionally relevant concern. In dreams people think about their main concerns, particularly those concerns they have been unable to solve by conscious thought alone, and try to develop and test plans [...] for dealing with them [...] From

this perspective, dreams may be viewed as simple but important messages that dreamers send themselves.

(Gazzillo et al., 2019, p. 3)

Dreams are therefore an adaptive resource in that they creatively
link problems and emotions with earlier memory traces and practice coping with previously unresolved situations by simulating
and testing possible solutions. In this respect, a higher level of
unconscious mental functioning is active in dreaming.

To summarize, it can be said that in various newer theories one
can observe a movement away from Freud's wish fulfillment
theory towards theories according to which dreams primarily
provide emotional regulation and problem solving.

The Kohutian perspective – The dream as a representation (and restoration) of the self

In Fiss's (1995) theory, every dream is a manifestation of a
(presumed) underlying self; the dream is given the function of
consolidating identity on the basis of this self, of promoting
self-development, maintaining or restoring it. This is already
very close to the view of self-psychology on the dream, as first
formulated by Kohut (1977). Although Kohut did not develop
a differentiated dream theory, he assigns the work with dreams
a central role in the analysis. In particular, he places a second
model of so-called self-state dreams alongside Freud's dream
model. Self-state dreams appear when the stability of the
structure of the ego is endangered and needs to be stabilized or
restored. He emphasizes that this act of representing the entire
inner-psychic situation in the dream is a way of countering the
endangerment of the personality structure – in that the name-
less fear in the dream is captured in an image. Dreams are
therefore part of the psyche's ability to self-regulate, which is
activated when its integrity is threatened. Stolorow (1978; Stolorow & Atwood, 1993) has taken this further and emphasized
that the dream image takes on the function of encapsulating
the threat to the personality structure by giving it a form, and
thus at the same time represents a repair of the damaged or

destabilized self. The function of the dream is therefore to protect the psychic organization through the reparative use of
concretization. This model leads to a way of working in the
analysis in which the attempt is no longer made to decipher the
latent dream content, but rather the focus is on a joint examination of the dream and how the dreamer's personal world and
inner situation are expressed in it. It is not only the symbolism
in the dream and the dreamer's associations with it that are
important here; interestingly, Stolorow also emphasizes the significance of the structure of the dream and the configurations
of self and objects that structure the dream narrative. In this
structural relationship between self and objects in the dream
lies an additional level of understanding on which the unconscious experiential structures of the person are expressed. The
dream is thus seen as a mirror of the dreamer's inner, subjective
universe. The parallels to Jung's view on the dream, especially
to his concept of the subjective level of interpretation, are clear.

Fosshage (1987) takes this even further in his theory, using neuroscientific and cognitive psychological research and models. For
him, the most important function of the dream is the development,
maintenance and re-establishment of psychic organization. By
creating images, the dream consolidates psychic developmental
processes or even foresees them while these developments are not
yet perceptible to the conscious mind. As an example of this, he
describes the case of a fifty-year-old analyst who was professionally
successful but lived a very emotionally restricted life. The image of
a red Porsche that she drives appears in her dreams. This dream
image alludes to her vital and emotionally lively side, whereby the
dream first announces this development while this impulse had not
yet arrived in her conscious life. In addition, the dream can take on
the function of restoring a psychological balance; for example, by
expressing suppressed emotions and impulses in dream images and
thus paving the way for them to reach the dreamer's consciousness.

Long before Kohut and other self-psychologists, however,
Fairbairn (1952) already had a similar view of dreams: Based on
his analytic experience, he came to view dreams as "dramatizations
or 'shorts' (in the cinematographic sense) of situations existing in
inner reality" (p. 99). The manifest dream content does not conceal

the actual meaning, rather it shows precisely the unconscious relationships between subpersonalities of the dreamer or from such subpersonalities to object representations.

Theoretical pluralism

This diversity of current theoretical concepts leads Bohleber (2012) in his overview of the state of psychoanalytic dream theories – parallel to the current view of the different psychoanalytic schools – to summarize that one must also speak of psychoanalytic pluralism with regard to dream interpretation. The mainstream has turned away from Freudian theory and made the manifest dream the object of investigation as the actual dream content. Freud's theory devalued the manifest dream and thus obscured the fact that it itself has an integrative function. Current dream interpretation in psychoanalysis has much more to do with the creation of meaning than with the uncovering of a latent unconscious meaning. However, Bohleber also emphasizes that central elements of Freud's theory have been confirmed by more recent research. Firstly, that primary-process thinking is at work in dreams, and secondly that unconscious motives and wishes in particular play an important role in dream production.

A certain convergence can be observed in the conception of dreams between the Freudian and Jungian schools in the developments described. Erikson (1955) already emphasized that there is no categorical difference between latent dream thoughts and manifest dream content, as was previously thought, which consequently also makes the methodology of decoding dream censorship obsolete. However, the psychotherapeutic dream work of psychoanalysis is thus already quite close to Jung's view that the dream expresses exactly what it says and that it is a self-image of the psyche. With particular reference to Jung's concept of interpreting the dream at the subject level, the (Freudian) psychoanalyst Ermann (2005) writes:

> The interpretation of dreams at the subject level is a particularly original contribution (by Jung) to dream theory. It has found its way into the treatment of dreams in all psychoanalytically based

therapeutic directions. [...] Freudian psychoanalysts are often no longer even aware that they are using a Jungian concept when they regard dream motifs as images of the self or parts of it.

(p. 40; transl. C.R.)

Dieckmann (1965) points out, however, that this idea can also be found in Freud:

Freud, very early on, in his book The interpretation of dreams (1900), saw that figures or events in dreams could be understood as projections or representations of the ego. This idea was developed later by Stekel into his theory of the functional meaning of dreams, and by Jung into the interpretations of dreams on the subjective level.

(p. 66)

The more recent view ascribes to the dream above all a communicative function in psychoanalytic treatment: Infantile object relationships are represented in the dream which also appear in the transference, but which can be made the subject of conversation via dream interpretation. Basically, every dream can (and must) be viewed as a commentary on the analytic relationship. In today's psychoanalytic interpretation of dreams, what the dream contributes as a communication (of the unconscious) to the therapeutic relationship and its further development within the psychotherapeutic process with a view to changes in the patient is regarded as central.

Moser (2003) attempts to summarize what all approaches have in common in the following formula:

The goal of dream work in the analytic situation is the adoption of the dream into the shared interpretative micro-world of analyst and analysand. The dream is a personal contribution to rethinking one's own situation in a preverbal language that is not readily accessible.

(p. 655; transl. C.R.)

Chapter 5

Psychotherapeutic work with dreams in other schools of therapy

Even though dream interpretation as a psychotherapeutic method certainly developed first in psychoanalysis, and is probably used most frequently here, other schools of therapy have also developed forms of working with dreams in psychotherapy or integrated them into their arsenal of methods (for an overview, see Hill & Knox, 2010; Giovanardi, 2021). First and foremost, Gestalt therapy should be mentioned here, although its work with dreams is closely based on psychoanalytical methods.

Even in cognitive behavioral therapy approaches have been developed that make working with dreams and their interpretation part of the therapeutic work; these approaches are very close to Jung's technique of working with dreams and active imagination (Hill & Rochlen, 2004). The approach of psychotherapy researcher Clara Hill is described below as an outstanding example. Hill is a psychotherapy researcher who works across different schools, and her interest in the topic of dreams was primarily to investigate the effectiveness of working with dreams for psychotherapy. Initially, she and her research group developed their own model of dream work (Cognitive-Experiential Dreamwork) from existing approaches, which was intended to be easy to learn (Hill, 1996). In summary, it includes:

1 Exploration: The dream is narrated, associations with the dream elements are collected and connections to waking life are explored.

DOI: 10.4324/9781003492078-6

2   Insight: The question "What does the dream mean?" is explored and the links to problems and memories of waking life are examined from this point of view.

3   Realization: The meaning of the dream constructed in this way is processed into suggestions for action in waking life.

In comparison with psychoanalytic dream theories, it is noticeable that in purely practical terms this methodology is very much in line with the basic features of Jungian dream work, even if important characteristics of Jungian work with dreams, e.g. amplification and compensation theory, are missing. In the meantime, Hill and colleagues have also developed an effective therapeutic procedure for the treatment of post-traumatic nightmares from this approach (Spangler & Hill, 2015).

In Carl Rogers' person-centered approach, it was also common practice to talk about dreams from the very beginning. However, there was neither an explicit theory nor a formulated methodology for interpreting dreams. It is only recently that textbooks on the person-centered approach have included explicit theoretical models for the use of dreams in psychotherapy:

> The organismic experience can often become more visible in dreams than in waking life, since the self-concept here is more open to its own unconscious organismic existence, so that the person is often, in a sense, ahead of himself here. They are already truer and more real here than corresponds to their own conscious self-perception and self-definition. At this (largely unconscious) level of the organismic self, the person is often smarter, more forward-looking, more creative and more imaginative than at the level of consciousness or the conceptual self.
>
> (Finke , Deloch & Stumm, 2019, p. 48; transl. C.R.)

The effect of the actualization tendency can be clearly seen in dreams. As the person is relieved of the pressure of the demands of reality during sleep, the "night side" of the person can be expressed, so to speak – in particular, less symbolized aspects of the person that are neglected by the conscious self-image. In this respect, the regulative function of the actualizing tendency, which has a balancing effect aimed at a holistic consideration of all aspects of the person, is unfolded in the dream. This is where the neglected opposite side, which is ignored by the self-concept, can direct its message of the organismic self to the consciousness. "The dream as the realm of the phantasmatic, the irrational and the imaginary is in a special way the stage on which the unconscious organismic existence can be presented" (Finke et al., 2019, p. 49). Specifically, dream events are understood here as representations of relational events and the dream figures as real persons. On the other hand, the figures presented in dreams can also be seen as different aspects of the dreamer's self. The person-centered approach refers to these two alternative perspectives as the relational perspective versus the self-perspective. The parallels to Jung's view are obvious; the authors explicitly refer to Jung but also borrow from other authors of the humanistic approach such as Fritz Perls (Perls et al., 2006) and Eugene Gendlin (1987).

Working with dreams in couple therapy

As in individual therapy, dreams are also used in couple therapy. Between 1990 and 1998, Baumgart and Hamburger set up the so-called dream workshop, which organized dream workshops at weekends for four to eight couples each (Traumwerkstatt, 1998). The course of a couple's dream session was as follows: One participant presents a dream and gives their own associations. Then the partner may add their associations to the dream and finally the whole group associates with the dream described and its images. At this point, it is less about an interpretation and more about personal ideas about the dream images. The group forms a resonance with the imagined dream and its unconscious content, which can also manifest itself in scenic acting. In this way, the unconscious of several people present is used to enrich and understand the dream content.

In her book which arose from her experiences in the aforementioned dream workshop, the systemic therapist Roth (2003) describes her approach to the inclusion of dreams in couples therapy using numerous case examples:

If a partner brings a dream into the couples therapy at my suggestion, I begin to form hypotheses about the meaning of the dream at this point in the treatment. I try to shed more light on the context in which a dream is brought into the treatment. Is the dream a kind of weapon against the partner or a peace offering? Is the dream a gift to the therapist or an offer of flirtation? [...] Can the dream intensify the couple's clinch or rather contribute to its relaxation? After I have developed hypotheses about the context of the dream, I try to test them and include the partner who did not contribute a dream. In the next step, I ask the couple what they can think of regarding the details of the dream and, as far as possible, I try to understand the dream myself. [...]

Some dreams describe a typical interaction between the couple in a scene that is worth going into. Almost slapstick-like scenes of a marriage are depicted in the dream and can be used wonderfully in the subsequent work with the couple. In other dreams, the wishes and fears of one partner in relation to the other can be recognized and worked out in the dream. Still others conceal themselves or the partner in symbolizations. [...] I try to find out with the couple what these symbolizations could mean. If necessary, I explain the stylistic device of dramatization in the dream, otherwise the resistance to deal with the dream is too great. For example, if a partner dreams of killing his wife, this does not mean that he really wants to kill her, but the dreamed murder is a dramatic staging of an aggressive impulse towards his wife. [...]

During dream processing in couple therapy, I don't interpret the dream directly, but try to play with it. By this I mean that as a therapist I pass the dream or parts of the dream to the partners like a ball and encourage both of them to contribute further ideas to their dream.

(Roth, 2003, p. 20f.)

The Jungian couple therapist Desteian (1989) also describes a way of working with dreams with partners: From the author's point of view, dreams reflect the relationship of the individual to the soul image. The soul image is projected onto the partner in the couple relationship and the therapeutic work now consists of detaching this projection from the partner again and individuating oneself. The dream work also serves to recognize shadow parts that have been split off in the relationship. Reintegration often takes place in the dream in such a way that the partner (in the dream) contacts these parts and re-evaluates them in a new and different way.

Chapter 6

Empirical dream research

It is interesting to note that empirical dream research also began with suggestions from psychoanalysis as early as 1917 by Otto Pötzl at the Department of Psychiatry in Vienna (Berner et al., 2018). This laboratory research was continued in Frankfurt by the psychoanalyst Leuschner (1999), among others.

Based on the discovery that dream sleep can be recognized in the sleeper by rapid movements of the pupils behind the closed eyelids (rapid eye movement: REM), this enabled an empirical approach to dreams. Whenever test subjects were awakened from REM sleep, they consistently reported intense dreams (Aserinsky & Kleitman, 1953). Subsequently, empirical dream research developed, the results of which can be followed above all in the two leading specialist journals *Dreaming* and *International Journal of Dream Research*. After an initial phase in which empirical dream researchers declared their opposition to psychoanalysis, a clear turnaround can be observed since the 1970s: Increasingly, psychoanalytic concepts are being taken seriously and no longer rejected a priori as unscientific. Beginning as early as the 1960s, empirical dream researchers even adopted psychoanalytic concepts in their own conceptions and systematically examined them (e.g. Hall & Van De Castle, 1966). In more recent overviews of dream research, there is appreciative reference to the contributions of psychoanalysis to the explanation of dreams (e.g. Schredl, 2007). In addition, a number of psychoanalysts are now also conducting systematic empirical dream research (e.g. Kramer & Glucksman, 2015).

DOI: 10.4324/9781003492078-7

REM sleep is important for the organism

Following the discovery of REM sleep and its connection to dreaming, a model of so-called sleep architecture was developed in related research (Solms, 2011). In this model, phases of more or less dreamless deep sleep alternate with REM sleep phases, the latter increasing towards the morning.

This model already provides an important insight for our questions: Before you can dream – i.e. before a REM sleep phase is experienced – you must first go through a phase of deep sleep. In this respect, one could say that it is not the dream that is the guardian of sleep but that sleep is a prerequisite for dreaming. This would initially refute Freud's view. Furthermore, REM sleep obviously has an important function for the organism.

In his systematic studies, Hartmann (1973) found that REM sleep deprivation resulted in irritability, concentration difficulties, and problems with interpersonal contact and impulse control. However, some test subjects felt better under REM sleep deprivation. This phenomenon is particularly well known in depressive patients. Even if REM sleep deprivation does not have such serious consequences as was originally assumed, numerous test subjects still experienced psychological restrictions and stress after several nights of REM sleep deprivation – apparently there are major inter-individual differences here. After a few days of deprivation, the organism makes up for the lost REM sleep (REM rebound), which indicates that the organism has a biological need for dream sleep. This assumption is also supported by the fact that REM sleep exerts the body and therefore consumes a lot of energy. It would be biologically pointless to catch up on such strenuous activity if it were not important for the functioning of the organism (Werner & Langenmayr, 2005).

Activation-synthesis theory

Hobson and McCarley (1971, 1977) discovered a region in the upper brain stem that controls the alternation between REM and non-REM sleep. They developed their "activation-synthesis theory" in a declared opposition to psychoanalytic concepts, according to which characteristic excitation waves emanate from the brain stem and activate the centers for vision, hearing and movement in the brain. The cortex tries to make sense of these random activations, and the result is the dreams experienced. This proved that dreams had no meaning. This theory dominated sleep and dream research for almost two decades. Does this mean that dreams have no meaning for psychological (waking) life?

Dreams are not senseless

The activation-synthesis theory of Hobson and McCarley (1971, 1977), according to which dreams arise from meaningless random activations of the brain, is now regarded as refuted in empirical sleep and dream research, partly because it has been established that dreaming also occurs outside of REM sleep (Foulkes, 1982a) and that many more brain regions are involved in triggering dreams than just the brain stem. This was proven above all by Solms' (2000) dream studies on brain-damaged patients. He was able to show that, depending on which brain regions were damaged, dream activity and REM sleep occur independently of each other, i.e. dreams are produced in different centers (for an overview of the debate between Hobson and Solms, see Solms, 2013b).

Solms' neuropsychoanalytic dream theory

REM sleep, controlled by cholinergic brainstem (pons) mechanisms, can only generate the psychological process of dreaming through the mediation of a second, dopaminergic forebrain mechanism. Solms demonstrated that dreaming can be manipulated by dopaminergic agonists and antagonists independently of REM frequency, duration and density and can be triggered by forebrain stimulation during non-REM sleep phases. He concludes that the "'REM-on' mechanism (like its various NREM equivalents) therefore stands outside the dream process itself, which is mediated by an independent, forebrain 'dream-on' mechanism" (Solms, 2011, p. 543). Through this clinical-anatomical evidence based on Freud's aphasia research, Solms (2011) was able to refute the above-mentioned thesis that dreaming is the brain's attempt to give meaning to senseless excitation storms from the brain stem and thus prove that dreams are not meaningless.

Solms' (2000, 2011) findings indicate that our dreaming is linked to the mesolimbic reward system. The release of dopamine in this regulatory circuit stimulates us to give in to our curiosity and longing and to repeat a rewarding activity. If this release of dopamine is a fundamental prerequisite for dreaming, it fulfills the function of a deep desire satisfaction (following Freud) of the organism for an inherent process such as dreaming, but without our willful awake-active intervention in the sense of goal-oriented motivated behavior (see Solms' definition above: "motivated behavior is precluded during sleep"). This is precisely what is made impossible because access to the motor system is blocked during sleep. Instead, motivated behavior only takes place in the imagination. At the same time, the ability to reflect is paralyzed in the front part of the limbic system during sleep, so that the visualized dream scenes are accepted uncritically and misinterpreted by the dreamer as real perceptions. The dream mechanism is a two-stage regressive process: First the higher brain regions of the perceptual system, which enable memory and abstract thinking, are activated at the occipital-temporal-parietal interface (sulcus lateralis), then the deeper regions that provide concrete images. The process of perception in dreams would thus run backwards: The abstract is transformed into concrete perception.

In addition, the claimed connection between eye movements and dreaming is questionable. It has been shown that not only REM sleep is dream sleep but that mental activities take place during the entire sleep (Foulkes, 1982a). Even though they make up about 20% of dream sleep, non-REM dreams have a different character than REM dreams: They are less fantastic and more similar to orderly thinking in the waking state; they do not promote creativity, but they do support learning and memory consolidation. REM versus non-REM dreams also reveal different aspects of personality (Vedfelt, 2017).

These findings have been combined in a new model: Here, a distinction is no longer made between two but three different states of consciousness, namely wakefulness, REM sleep (dreaming) and non-REM sleep (deep sleep, although dreaming also occurs here). The above model of sleep architecture would imply that people sleep less deeply when dreaming than in so-called deep sleep, which is actually not empirically true: It is relatively difficult to wake a dreamer. In the new model, the three states of consciousness are differentiated on the basis of three dimensions: Activation, sensory input and the predominant neurotransmitters. The fascinating result is that dreaming is a separate state of consciousness that cannot be equated with sleep. In terms of mental activation, dreaming is completely comparable to thinking while awake but is based on other predominant neurotransmitters and, in particular, does not process sensory input from the outside but exclusively from within the organism – the latter in particular would support the psychoanalytical views on dreaming.

It is now assumed that mental activity continues during sleep and that experiences from waking life continue to be processed here but that different brain regions and functions are involved during sleep than during wakefulness. "Earlier assertions that dream content arises purely by chance and has no connection to the dreamer's waking life are no longer tenable," states one of the leading dream researchers (Schredl, 2006, p. 50).

Continuity between waking and dreaming

Instead, a general continuity between mental activity in waking life and dream sleep is assumed. This so-called continuity theory of waking and dreaming is actually one of the most prominent theories in dream research today and is considered to be well documented (Schredl, 2015). This means that the way a person's mind functions in a dream is not fundamentally different from the way it functions while awake. This continuity hypothesis was first formulated by Hall and Nordby (1972) on the basis of their content-analytic studies of dream series (see below): "The desires and fears that determine our actions and thoughts in everyday life also determine what we will dream about" (p. 104). Interestingly, these authors also cite Freud as a proponent of this thesis, namely by referring to his theory of day residues, according to which experiences of the previous day represent crystallization points for the dreams of the night. This hypothesis is now well supported by a whole series of empirical studies by various dream researchers (for overviews, see Domhoff, 1996; Schredl, 2015). A mathematical model has even been calculated that can be used to determine the relationship between events of the day and the probability of their occurrence in the dreams of the following night (Schredl, 2003).

In concrete terms, this also means that in people with mental disorders, these psychological characteristics are also reflected in their dreams; for example, depressive patients have significantly more "masochistic" themes in their dreams than healthy subjects. A close quantitative correlation can even be established: In depressed patients, the severity of their depressive symptoms correlates directly with the intensity of negatively perceived emotions in dreams and changes in parallel with the improvement of their emotional state during therapy (Schredl, 2015). The president of the International Society for Dream Research, Deirdre Barrett, summarizes this as follows: "I believe that dreams are just thinking in a very different biochemical and electrophysiological state" (Barrett, 2015, p. 91).

Meaningful connections between waking life and dream content

While empirical dream research, based on the discovery of REM sleep, was primarily psychophysiologically oriented, later research focused on the content and meaning of dreams. Kramer, Hlasny, Jacobs and Roth (1976) used a sorting procedure to investigate whether dreams are meaningful. They came to the clear conclusion "that dreams are, as depth psychologists have assumed, orderly nonrandom events and that they reflect day-to-day changes in the life of an individual" (p. 780). In their review of dream research, Kramer and Glucksman (2015) even summarize the current position of empirical dream research as follows:

> The fundamental assumption in dream research is that dreaming represents an altered form of consciousness under the specific conditions of sleep. We believe, on the basis of extensive empirical evidence, that the dream report reflects the psychology of the dreamer, both current and long-term aspects of the dreamer's emotional state, i.e. both in terms of current states and personality traits. [...] Dreams are ordered and non-random events, so that the possibility exists that they have meaning.
>
> (p. XII)

Fisher and Greenberg (1977, 1996), in their large-scale reviews of the empirical testing of Freud's theory, list a wealth of empirical findings that demonstrate a connection between a person's waking life and dream activity:

- People who have experienced natural disasters are more likely to have nightmares.
- Pregnant women dream about babies significantly more often than non-pregnant women.
- There are many parallels between the results of projective tests and the manifest dream content.
- If test subjects are exposed to different foreign languages in a sleep laboratory before falling asleep, these are systematically reflected in their dreams.

These are just a few examples. The empirical dream researcher Foulkes (1982a, p. 312) writes: "No one who has experience in collecting, researching and interpreting dreams can doubt that dreams often express a person's basic state of mind and make their problems visible".

Ermann (2005) summarizes: "Against this background, everything speaks for and nothing against ascribing psychological motives to dreams and assigning them a meaning that confirms their psychotherapeutic value" (Ermann, 2005, p. 66; transl. C. R.). In his overview of experimental dream research, Schredl (2006) summarizes the empirical results on the connection between waking and dream experience. According to this, people who played a role in the dreamer's waking life on the previous day appear significantly more frequently in dreams than other events that occurred longer ago. In particular, events in waking life that represented real stress for the person concerned (i.e. were not experimentally induced) often appeared as dream content, e.g. upcoming surgery, a divorce or a kidnapping. Overall, emotional involvement increases the likelihood of dreaming about a waking event, such as the rejection of food in the dreams of anorexia patients. In general, therefore, dreams reflect events in waking life, especially if they are emotionally significant for the person. Vedfelt (2017) summarizes this in his review as follows: "Dreams deal with matters important to us" (p. 46).

In turn, dreams have an effect on waking life. The most common effect is the influence on mood the next day (Schredl, 2000). In an interesting diary study, which was very similar to the usual practice of keeping a dream diary in analytical psychotherapy, Köthe and Pietrowsky (2001) were able to show that anxiety, ability to concentrate and self-esteem were significantly impaired after nights with nightmares. Nightmares were defined as dreams with a strong negative affect that lead to awakening. On the other hand, more recent studies have shown that nightmares can have a positive effect on coping strategies in the waking state and thus also have beneficial effects (Picchioni & Hicks, 2009).

Chapter 7

The functions of dreams

There are several theories from empirical dream researchers that attribute an adaptive function for the psyche to dreaming (Moffitt, Kramer & Hoffmann, 1993). In their mastery hypothesis, Wright and Koulack (1987) propose that cognitive activity in dreams is of the same nature as in waking life and that solutions to problems are sought in dreams.

Since it can be shown that the morning mood varies less than the evening mood, the theory of mood regulation (Kramer & Hoffmann, 1993) states that dreaming processes emotional experiences and balances the mood (Kuiken & Sikora, 1993). Hartmann's theory (1996) assumes that dreaming allows a different type of information processing: Since divergent thinking with far-reaching associations predominates in REM sleep, creative solutions are more likely to be possible here than in the task-related convergent thinking of the waking state. Spitzer, Walder and Clarenbach (1993) were able to experimentally confirm that a mode of far-reaching associations does indeed predominate in REM sleep.

In his studies on the processing of trauma in dreams, Hartmann (1998) was able to show that the dream content is initially completely determined by the trauma but is then increasingly symbolized and that dreaming actually has an autotherapeutic function. Dreams perform the function of integrating unresolved affects into a context of experiential knowledge in such a way that the post-traumatic affects are alleviated.

DOI: 10.4324/9781003492078-8

Memory consolidation

Empirical studies increasingly indicate that REM sleep in particular is essential for the formation and consolidation of memory content and thus indirectly a prerequisite for the functioning of consciousness (Hallschmid & Born, 2006). In a famous study by Crick and Mitchison (1983), the theory was put forward that dreams are particularly important for forgetting irrelevant information and are therefore of crucial importance for the functioning of consciousness.

> In the central nervous system, the same neuronal networks are used for both the storage and acute processing of stimuli. As these networks cannot simultaneously consolidate freshly encoded memory content and acutely process external stimuli, the actual consolidation process takes place during sleep. The sleep state offers optimal conditions for processing freshly encoded memory traces 'offline' again, stabilizing them and integrating them into long-term memory content. Neuropsychologically, different memory systems can be distinguished, which store different information and are influenced by sleep in different ways. A number of studies show that declarative memory formation, which is dependent on the hippocampus, benefits above all from periods of sleep in which delta sleep predominates. In contrast, procedural and emotional memory formation, which are not hippocampally mediated, appear to be supported more strongly in sleep rich in REM sleep. Memory consolidation during sleep is probably based on a covert reactivation of those neuronal networks that have already been used to encode the relevant information during wakefulness.
>
> (Hallschmid & Born, 2006, p. 101)

Emotion regulation

As mentioned, dreams have a clearly noticeable mood-balancing effect, at least in the morning; they apparently regulate affects and emotions. Rüther and Gruber-Rüther (2000; see also Rodenbeck,

Gruber-Rüther & Rüther, 2006) attempt to place affect processing in dreams in a theoretical framework. They start from the fact that during REM sleep the inhibitory influence of serotonergic connections on the frontal cortex comes to a complete standstill, weakening its central and organizing control. This causes an associative loosening of brain functions, whereby existing affective patterns can be recalled and new patterns can be playfully tried out due to the high interchangeability of individual affects. "When new affect patterns are successfully tried out in the dream experience, old patterns can be overwritten and new affect patterns can be selected and neurally fixed instead" (Rodenbeck et al., 2006, p. 121).

Cartwright (1996) found that women who had dreamed about their ex-husband more often than others after their divorce were mentally healthier than the rest of the group after one year. In a further study, Cartwright , Luten, Young, Mercer and Bears (1998) were able to show that sleep has an affect-stabilizing effect: In healthy subjects with a higher evening depression score, negative affects dominated in the first half of the night; the second half of the night was dominated by positive affects. This means that sleep, especially affect-rich dream sleep, i.e. REM sleep, has a healing effect on mild mood deterioration. This could be explained by a mechanism similar to the above affect hypothesis, according to which negative affect can be processed in dreams by trying out new positive affective patterns and, if successful, consolidating them. Studies point in the same direction, which, as already mentioned, shows that nightmares have a positive effect on coping strategies in the waking state (Picchioni & Hicks, 2009). Cartwright (1991, 2005) also summarizes her many years of studies to the effect that dreams clearly have a stress-reducing, emotion-regulating and coping-promoting function. In a review of the current state of research on the emotion-regulating function of dreams, Nielsen and Lara-Carrasco (2007, p. 274) state:

In sum, evidence from a variety of types of studies supports the notion of an emotion regulation function of dreaming and the more specific suggestion that dream characters and their emotion-laden interactions with the dream self may mediate this regulatory effect.

Hartmann (1995, 1998), who has studied the autotherapeutic function of dreams in traumatization, is considered one of the strongest proponents of this hypothesis. Hartmann shows that in the period shortly after the traumatic event it is re-experienced in the dream like a movie, and the event appears unchanged in the dream. Some time after the event, however, there are changes in the dream: The place or the people involved are changed, and finally the real events are partially replaced by symbolic representations. Hartmann assumes that the dream helps with these change processes by contextualizing the emotions, i.e. in the dream – in a safe place where no new sensory input takes place – new connections are created and the violent emotionality is thus calmed and integrated.

Nielsen and Levin (2007) even assume that there is an anxiety extinction function in dreams. On the one hand, there is an increased accessibility to fearful memories in dreams, but these are then normally reorganized in the dream and combined with non-frightening characteristics. This function fails in nightmares.

Threat Simulation Theory (TST)

In recent years, a new theory has become prominent, elaborated in particular by Revonsuo, Tuominen and Valli (2015). This theory is based on the universal distribution of certain types of nightmares and assumes that dreams simulate typical dangers in the world of early humans in order to prepare the dreamer for coping with corresponding dangerous situations (hence the name "threat simulation theory"). Dreaming is understood here as an evolutionary cognitive ability that enables people to anticipate and practice coping with threatening situations, even in their sleep. This in turn could explain quite well why dreams often contain threatening situations – including bizarre elements such as menacing animals or monsters – which have long since ceased to be part of the reality of modern dreamers' lives. Other authors also argue that the function of dreaming is to provide us with a field for experimentation and learning in order to mentally simulate and stimulate our physical, intellectual and social abilities and thus psychologically prepare us for what we encounter in real life (usually in an attenuated form). Against this background, it is also argued that the dream type in which the dream ego is threatened or attacked represents a universal prototype of human dreams (see also the findings of "Structural Dream Analysis" below).

Promotion of insight

The specific question of whether (dream) sleep promotes insight was investigated by Wagner, Gais, Haider, Verleger and Born (2004). In their experiment, the test subjects had to work on a so-called number reduction task in which a hidden rule had to be recognized. In a training phase, the test subjects familiarized themselves with the task. Although this phase was too short to be able to recognize the relatively complex hidden rule, it created a mental representation of the task in memory. The experimental group then slept for around eight hours while two control groups remained awake. After ten hours, further blocks of the task had to be completed. It was found that more than twice as many subjects in the experimental group had gained insight into the hidden rule than in the control groups. Based on the experiment, it can be concluded that sleep does more than just strengthen memory traces; it leads to a restructuring of mental representations. It could therefore be shown that the improved insight ability was not due to the brain continuing to practice the task while asleep, so to speak, but because a combinatorial performance was apparently prepared during sleep: "This reactivation [of memory contents during sleep, author's note] can lead to a restructuring and thus to a qualitative change in the corresponding memory representation" (Hallschmid & Born, 2006, p. 101). This would be clear evidence that in dreams larger and also unconscious areas of the psyche can work together in a coordinated manner and thus a larger amount of information or processing capacity is available than in waking consciousness, which also makes significantly more creative insights possible. It has been proven that more brain systems are active simultaneously in dreams than in the waking state (McCarley & Hobson, 1979). For a more recent overview of this aspect, see Edwards, Ruby, Malinowski, Bennett and Blagrove (2013).

Problem solving

A connection between the amount of REM sleep and the ability to solve new or difficult tasks has also been demonstrated (Fiss, 1979). REM sleep consolidates important cognitive functions such as learning, problem solving, memory and coping mechanisms. So far, however, only De Koninck et al. (2003) have shown that it is also necessary to dream about what needs to be learned in order to achieve the memory-consolidating and insight-promoting effect.

It can therefore be concluded that all recent empirically based dream theories view dreaming as an information-processing activity that is not random, chaotic or meaningless, but rule-governed. Dreams are not only related to waking life experiences and problems; they also process them in a purposeful and apparently useful way. The dream researcher Hall (1966) summarizes this insight succinctly: "Dreaming is essentially a creative process, [...] the product of good hard thought" (p. 57).

Dreaming and creativity

One of Jung's most important statements about dreams was that they promote creativity and bring creative impulses to the consciousness that the consciousness alone would not be capable of. Jung liked to mention the example of the chemist Kekulé, who, according to his own statement, recognized the structure of the benzene ring through a dream image in which the molecules danced together in a circle. However, this example is questioned today, as Kekulé only reported this dream many years after his discovery (Schredl, 2006). There are, however, numerous other well-documented examples of the promotion of creativity through dreams. For example, numerous artists, including Salvador Dalí, Ingmar Bergman, Carlos Saura and Federico Fellini, are known to have translated dreams into their art. Paul McCartney heard the melody of the Beatles song "Yesterday" in a dream and was initially surprised that it was not a familiar tune. In science, the structure of the periodic table, the invention of the sewing machine and the deciphering of Babylonian cuneiform writing were inspired by dreams (Schredl, 2006).

In addition to these individual case reports, there are also systematic empirical studies on the contribution of dreams to creativity. Creativity here means receiving an idea in a dream that has an effect on waking life, e.g. a change in one's own behavior. Kuiken and Sikora (1993) and Schredl (2000) report that in student samples 20–28% of participants stated that they received creative impulses from dreams at least twice a year. In another study (Schredl, 2006), 7.8% of all documented dreams contained a creative element, with certain personality traits, such as the person's dream recall ability, visual imagination and "thin boundaries" apparently promoting the occurrence and use of creative dream elements. An example of a creative impetus for problem solving reported in this research is: "My PC was broken and I was dreaming about how best to fix it. I woke up the next morning and it was clear how I could get it working again" (Schredl, 2006, p. 61). Based on his studies, Schredl even recommends: "Particularly in creative professions or, for example, in complex motor skills, targeted training in dreams could have a useful effect on the rest of waking life" (p. 61). The dream researcher Barrett (2001), far from being a follower of psychoanalytic dream theories, has presented an extensive compilation of stories and experience reports on dream-based creative problem solving in science and culture. As an empirical researcher, she only selected reports whose credibility could be verified and analyzed them as part of a systematic study. In doing so, she came across numerous scientists and researchers who systematically use their dreams when working on professional problems. For example, she describes architects who walked through buildings in their dreams and memorized their characteristics in order to immediately enter them into their architectural designs the next day (Barrett, 2015). In addition to this collection of reports, Barrett has conducted systematic laboratory studies on the conditions under which waking life problems are creatively processed in dreams. These conditions can be specified. Pagel (2015) was able to prove in an empirical study with filmmakers that they had nightmares significantly more often than the general population but were also able to use them more often for their creative work.

Summary: A contemporary theory of the function of dreams

From today's perspective, the connection between dreams, memory and problem solving can be formulated as follows (see Windt, 2015): Experiences of the day, especially those with emotional significance or even stressful affects, are reactivated from short-term memory storage during dreaming and compared with earlier experiences from long-term memory; in particular, how similar experiences and conflicts were resolved or overcome in earlier situations. In this respect, problems are actually processed and, to a certain extent, resolved during dreaming, so that the processed content can then be stored in long-term memory and does not place any further strain on mental functioning in everyday life. If this is not successful, the dream may lead to waking and is experienced or at least remembered as a nightmare. This processing of memory content in dreams is therefore a highly structured, rule-governed and targeted procedure that largely takes place unconsciously and coordinates various mental functional areas but which can only take place if no new mental input occurs, as is the case in the waking state (Vedfelt, 2017).

The fact that these processes are important for the organism and that dreaming is functional in this respect is also shown by REM sleep deprivation (Hartmann, 1973; Dement, 1966): Increased aggressive and sexual activation, poorer adaptability, concentration disorders, memory impairment, learning difficulties, a reduced ability to cope with stress and lower mental stability are then found. If stress-inducing tasks are presented in the sleep laboratory before falling asleep, this leads to an increase in the duration of REM sleep. If dreams are dealt with intensively – for example, psychotherapeutically – this leads to an improvement in well-being. Conversely, the number of threatening or aggressive dream contents increases if the person has previously been exposed to threatening events while awake.

In summary, it can therefore be said that dreaming has a regulatory function for the organism and in particular for mental functioning. Most prominent dream theories today agree that dreaming contributes to problem solving and coping with everyday demands (for an overview, see Barrett & McNamara, 2007).

The Contemporary Theory of Dreaming by **Ernest Hartmann (2010)**

1   Dreaming is a form of mental functioning: Dreaming is not alien to conscious thought, not material in a foreign language and not separable from other forms of mental functioning. It represents one end of a continuum of mental functioning, with focused waking thought at one end and through fantasy, daydreaming and reverie to dreaming at the other end.

2   Dreaming is hyperconnective: Connections are made more easily in dreaming than in waking, and these connections are broader and looser. Dreaming avoids structured and learned material. Dreaming always involves new connections between existing mental content, so it is creative, not simply repetitive.

3   The connections are not random: They are driven by the dreamer's emotions, in the sense that the central image of the dream is a pictorial representation of the dreamer's emotion or emotional concerns.

4   The form or language of the dream is primarily pictorial metaphor: This is not restricted to the dream, however, but is a form of thinking that also occurs in the waking state, which is less serially processive and less task-oriented, functioning less according to formal rules and less constrained. This system correlates with the default mode network: This default network of the brain is active when we are not focusing on something, but relaxing, not taking in sensory input, daydreaming, etc. It has vague functional rules, e.g. establishes associative links according to approximate or metaphorical similarity, is guided by emotions (the parallels to Freud's hypothesis of primary-process thinking in dreams are obvious).

5   Functions of dreaming: This broad establishment of connections via emotions has an adaptive function, whereby new material is woven into existing structures – new experiences are gradually connected and integrated into existing memory systems. Dreams help to build a meaningful emotional memory system, which forms the basis of the individual self. This function is fulfilled even if the dream is not remembered. When the dream is remembered, these broad connections take on an adaptive function in increasing self-knowledge and insight as well as creativity.

6   Function of the continuum from waking to dreaming: The fact
     that the mental system has this continuum is also adaptive, i.e.
     sometimes focused waking thinking is necessary, sometimes more
     associative, broader and looser thinking – and we do the latter in
     both dreams and daydreams.

Chapter 8

The empirical investigation of the content of dreams

For a long time, the content dimension of dreams was not systematically investigated. There was only a wealth of individual case reports from therapeutic processes, primarily from the psychoanalytic field. This changed with the research of Calvin Hall (1966), who was initially trained as a Freudian psychoanalyst but from the mid-1960s headed his own institute for empirical dream research. In *The Content Analysis of Dreams*, Hall and Van de Castle (1966) developed a systematic scientific method that met the criteria of objectivity, reproducibility of results, quantifiability and generalizability in order to research the content aspect of dreams. The basis is a comprehensive classification system with which individual dreams can be described and categorized. The dream is treated like a text and divided into individual segments, which can then be categorized in the classification system. The classification system provides categories for settings, people appearing, actions and emotions in the dream, e.g. how often men versus women appear and aggressive or sexual actions take place, etc. In addition, the method of contingency analysis was developed (Hall & Nordby, 1972), with which recurring connections between a person's dream elements can be recorded. In long-term studies, Hall and his colleagues used this classification system to examine dream series spanning several years and involving a wide variety of test subjects. They were able to show that the people, objects, actions and themes appearing in the dreams remained the same over a long period of time. The content of a person's dreams is therefore not random but shows a high degree of consistency even over long periods of time.

DOI: 10.4324/9781003492078-9

Interestingly, universal gender differences have been identified: Women are more passive in their dreams, whereas men are more often active; they run, drive cars, swim, dance, play ball, climb and do heavy work. Another universal difference, which is already significant from the age of six, is that in male dreams there are on average two men for every woman, whereas in female dreams the ratio is even. Aggression towards other men is also more common in male dreams, whereas in female dreams it is more common between men and women. Gender-specific differences can already be seen in children: Girls behave more socially in their dreams than boys and describe the faces of the people in the dream more often. Boys, on the other hand, are more likely to describe external aspects of the dream objects, such as their size or speed. These gender differences have been confirmed in numerous follow-up studies (see Fisher & Greenberg, 1977). However, more recent reviews argue that the differences found could rather be a consequence of gender-specific differences in the socialization of reporting dreams. In general, the more recent literature makes a stronger distinction between the dream and the dream report, and different types of dream reports (Windt, 2015). For example, it has been shown that the frequency with which emotions are reported in dreams increases tenfold when subjects are specifically asked about them. Simple coding methods would therefore dramatically underestimate the emotions that occur (Windt, 2015, p. 88).

Dream-based personality diagnostics

With the development of his classification method for examining dreams, Hall initiated extensive research into the content of dreams. As Hall's approach to dreams is not based on theoretical assumptions such as psychoanalytical approaches, it has been used extensively in scientific psychology. Hall's research approach was able to prove with scientific precision that dreams are not random products but that their content is systematically linked to the personality of the dreamer and their waking life and that a relatively valid personality diagnosis of the person can even be derived from the analysis of the content of dreams. Central life themes or problems of the dreamer can be determined from the dreams alone

(Hall & Nordby, 1972). For example, the authors describe a young woman who provided 61 dreams from her 32 months of psychotherapy. With the help of the classification system, the most important themes of her dream life could be determined: Men, sex, marriage, divorce, pregnancy, contraception and abortion. The data provided by the treating therapist showed that the patient wanted a husband and children on the one hand but feared that her body would be alienated, defiled and destroyed by the sexual act and pregnancy on the other.

In many other cases, Hall was able to show a clear connection between the themes of the dreams and the personality and psychic life of the person with the help of the objective classification of the dreams alone, without using a dream interpretation theory. This of course contradicts Freud's theory, which assumes a distortion of dream content through dream work. Partly as a result of these findings, the above-mentioned movement towards emphasizing the importance of the manifest dream content has emerged in psychoanalytic dream theories.

These connections between the dreamer's waking life and the content of their dreams go so far that the relative frequency of aggressive versus friendly interactions between the dreamer and a given person in their dreams can be used to predict the dreamer's actual waking attitude towards that person with a high degree of accuracy (Domhoff, 2003).

These correlations can also be confirmed from a developmental psychology perspective. Children dream about animals significantly more often than adults (Hall, 1966): Children under the age of four dream about animals in 51% of their dreams, children aged five to seven still dream about animals in 37% of all dreams. In adults, on the other hand, animals only appear in 7.5% of all dreams. The frequency of animal dreams decreases continuously as the child gets older. It is very interesting to note that those children who dream about animals more frequently than average, even at the age of seven, have lower social skills than the average for their age group. Children also dream of frightening animals more frequently than adults (28% versus 7%), whereby the animals appear to be increasingly tamed and controllable as the child gets older. These findings can be well explained by psychoanalytical dream theories: Especially in children, who are fundamentally not yet as in control of their psychological functions and cannot reflect as adults can, threatening animals in dreams in particular could symbolize the impulses and affects that cannot yet be controlled, which are experienced by the (dream) ego as a threat to its autonomy. The connection between lower social skills and more frequent animal dreams would confirm this. The fact that the actions of the dream ego in dreams reflect the strength of the ego and the capacity for reflection and control is also confirmed by the studies of Foulkes (1999), who showed that it takes up to thirteen years for the human ability to dream to be fully developed, parallel to cognitive and emotional development. According to him, children only have short, emotionally neutral dreams without complicated actions. As a rule, there is no dream ego in these dreams; this only emerges in dreams around the age of seven.

Barrett (1996) was able to prove in people with multiple personality disorder that the diagnostically known split-off subpersonalities of the patients appeared in their dreams as persons, some of whom even gave the dream ego helpful hints for waking life. The author interprets this as proof of the correctness of Jung's concept of the subject level in that personality parts can appear as persons in dreams and give the dreamer helpful hints. She was also able to confirm this finding for healthy subjects in a series of further studies and states: "Dreaming is the only state in which most of us interact with aspects of ourselves as discrete other people" (Barrett, 2015, p. 86).

Windt (2015) lists a number of other scientific approaches that systematically analyze the content and structure of dreams. All of these studies support the findings described above that the content of dreams is systematically related to the personality of the dreamer and their significant psychological themes (see in particular the overview in Perogamvros, Dang-Vu, Desseiles & Schwartz, 2013).

Patterns in the dreams of one night

Kramer (1964) was able to show that the themes of a night's dreams develop according to a certain pattern for the same person. In the first half of the night, the dreams deal with current experiences; in the second half they tend to deal with events from the dreamer's past and towards morning they return to current themes. Often only one single theme is dealt with in the dreams of a single night, in forms ranging from unpleasant and tense to relaxing. At the very least, the movement from current to past events over the course of the night would confirm Freud's view of the connection between daytime residue and biographically induced unconscious conflicts. Cartwright (1977) was also able to show that morning dreams have a problem-solving tendency. She confirms the patterns found by Kramer and brings them into a context: The first dreams of the night take up a current topic and problematize it, the following dreams reach back into the dreamer's past in order to search for problem-solving possibilities there, and the last dreams before waking then contain attempts to solve the problem. Like Hall (1966), Cartwright (1977) also found a high degree of continuity in a person's dream themes over long periods of time. Levin (1990) also found this in his review. However, Cartwright was also able to show that the dream themes of a person who takes serious steps to change their life – for example, by undergoing psychotherapy – do not continue but change.

What role does the day residue play?

Freud had already emphasized in his theory that emotionally significant elements from the events of the previous day are taken up again in dreams. This concept, known as day residue, is supported by practically all schools of dream interpretation. It can be empirically proven that dreams at night do indeed usually refer to at least one event from the previous day (Vedfelt, 2017). On the other hand, such elements can still appear in dreams five to seven days after the event. As described above, it is assumed that this serves to consolidate memory. In a recent review of relevant research, Horton and Malinowski (2015) found that dreaming plays a crucial role in the formation of autobiographical memory. Dreams organize memories into narratives in which recent episodic memories are aligned with older memory content. Forming narratives is apparently, according to the authors, fundamental to the way the brain organizes and integrates experience – and this happens in waking as well as in sleeping.

However, the reference of dreams to past events can be differentiated even further than simply stating that they pick up on remnants of the day. Schredl (2006) was able to prove that dreams at the beginning of the night tend to pick up on the remnants of the day in the sense that they refer to events from the previous day, while dreams from the later phases of the night refer to events from further back. Vedfelt (2017) distinguishes five different time references of dreams to events in waking life:

1 nearby events and daytime remnants
2 current life situations in the general sense, including personal relationships
3 life-historical events and relationship patterns of childhood;
4 the dreamer's age and related phases of life
5 future life transitions and life phases (p. 105)

Chapter 9

The effects of working with dreams in psychotherapy

So far, empirical results on the effect and function of dreams in general have been considered. Clara Hill investigated the direct effect of working with dreams in psychotherapy. In a previous study (Fiss, 1979), two groups of test subjects were formed: The first group was woken up during all REM sleep phases and asked to recount their dreams and then discuss them again with the experimenter the next morning. The second group was woken up during non-REM phases. Both groups received the same amount of therapeutic conversations in parallel to the sleep lab sessions. The subjects who were able to remember their dreams the next morning and discuss them with the investigator made significantly greater progress in the accompanying therapy, as measured by standardized tests and independent clinical assessment.

Clara Hill's model of dream work

Since 1992, Clara Hill's research group has been conducting systematic studies on the effects of therapeutic work with dreams. Initially, a specific model of dream work was extracted from the existing approaches which was intended to be easy to learn (Hill, 1996). This model of dream work has already been described above.

In one study, this methodology was used over a period of six weeks (Cogar & Hill, 1992). No strong effects were found, but the subjects stated that they had developed a greater understanding of themselves. Six weeks is, of course, a short period of time compared to the usual periods used in psychoanalysis, so no stronger

DOI: 10.4324/9781003492078-10

effects would have been expected here. A comparative study with different conditions of dream work (interpretation of one's own dream, interpretation of another person's dream, work with a waking event) showed that the subjects rated the work with their own dream as more profound and effective than in the control conditions (Hill, Diemer, Hess, Hillyer & Seeman, 1993). In this study, three possible explanations for the effects of dream interpretation were examined:

1   the importance of the dream itself;
2   projection onto the dream;
3   the interpretation process

The explanation regarding the importance of the dream itself (1.) assumes that dreams are a meaningful reflection of unconscious or waking conflicts and can have a problem-solving function. A dream interpretation should have several effects: Sessions in which dreams are interpreted should be seen by clients as deep and valuable, issues should gain more clarity, and there should be positive and less negative emotionality. Even though negative feelings may be aroused during a dream interpretation, the discovery of new insights should result in a positive feeling.

An alternative explanation (2.) for the effect of dream interpretation is that we create arbitrary meaning from meaningless symbols. Consequently, the real dream could be meaningless, but we could create meaning by reading something into it.

Another explanation (3.) is that the process of interpretation itself may be the useful part of dream work in therapy.

The study compared the effects on session quality, insight and emotion of three conditions: Interpretation of one's own dream, interpretation of another person's dream, and interpretation of one's own experience (not dream). 60 subjects were assigned to the three conditions. Each of the five therapists conducted one-hour sessions with four volunteers in each of the three conditions, for a total of twelve sessions per therapist. The results showed that the interpretation of one's own dream led to a higher rating of the quality of the session by the clients compared to the other conditions. This showed that the effect of dream interpretation is caused by more factors than just the process of interpretation. In addition, the interpretation of one's own dream led to higher ratings regarding insight than the other conditions. This shows that the effect of dream interpretation is not only influenced by projection (Hill et al., 1993). With regard to the question of which elements of dream work are most effective, it was shown that collecting associations is more helpful than simply describing the dream (Hill, Nakayama & Wonnell, 1998). Making connections to waking life proved to be the most effective (Hill, Diemer & Heaton, 1997). Working in dream groups with the model also showed a positive effect on self-esteem in women who were going through or had gone through a divorce compared to a control group (Falk & Hill, 1995). The methodology was also judged to be at least as effective as problem-oriented work (Diemer, Lobell, Vivino & Hill, 1996).

One result is particularly interesting for Jung's dream work: In one study (Hill & Spangler, 2007), a distinction was made between two conditions of dream work in the insight phase. In the first, the dream was related to aspects of waking life; in the second, the elements of the dream were interpreted as parts of the dreamer's personality or self (!) – in Jungian terms, one could therefore speak of an interpretation at the object level versus an interpretation at the subject level. Both conditions proved to be equally effective for gaining insights that lead to new ways of acting in waking life.

In a summarizing review of the studies of their research group, Hill and Spangler (2007; see also Spangler & Hill, 2015) state that

• Clients consistently rate psychotherapeutic sessions in which dreams are worked with higher than sessions in which other issues are worked with.
• Working with the client's own dreams and not just with waking life experiences or problems brings clear benefits. This cannot be attributed solely to the therapist's attention or projection processes.
• Subjects who consciously remember their dreams and can then discuss them with the therapist benefit more from the therapy. In other words, it is not enough just to dream; making the unconscious conscious is what makes sense.

- It makes sense to make associations and connections to waking life.
- Clients gain valuable insights through therapeutic work with dreams. This finding is consistent across many different methods of recording insight. It shows that clients do not suddenly find insights that they did not have before, but that, often starting from a good understanding of their dreams, they can continuously increase the benefits of dream work for their lives through the therapeutic sessions.
- These insights are not only cognitive but also lead to changes in the client's life. It is precisely this that clients experience as particularly valuable. However, the highest degree of effectiveness is only achieved when the dream work includes all three phases mentioned above.
- It was also measured whether the insights gained from the dream work actually relate to specific problems in the client's life. Not only is this the case, but it can even be determined that the effects of the problem focused on in the dream change significantly in the person's waking life after a single session of dream work (e.g. the person experiences themselves as significantly more competent in dealing with the problem).
- Even a reduction in symptoms can be observed after dream work; e.g. a decrease in depressive symptoms and an increase in subjective well-being.
- It is sensible and useful to interpret dream elements as personality traits of the dreamer according to the interpretation at the subject level.
- For effective work with dreams, it is particularly important to get the client to explicitly develop new options for action from the understanding of the dream. This is not usually the case in the more reserved psychoanalytical approach.

With regard to the contextual conditions of successful dream work, Hill and Spangler (2007) found that positive effects were associated with a high evaluation of the dreams and the dream work on the part of the client as well as with their commitment. It is also interesting to note that the more the therapist identifies with their model of dream work and adheres to its methodology in their practical work, the more positive the effect of the dream work. Spangler and Hill have now also developed an effective therapeutic procedure for the treatment of post-traumatic nightmares from this approach, which they have been able to prove (Spangler & Hill, 2015).

Current research on the relation between (the effects of) psychotherapy and dreams

As pointed out above, the findings of empirical dream research (Barrett & McNamara, 2007) can be summarized insofar as they relate to psychotherapy: In the dream, the brain is in a mode where it does not have to process new input but can use larger capacities for working on problems and finding creative solutions. The dreaming mind especially focuses on experiences in waking life that have emotional meaning for the dreamer and can find solutions for problems more readily compared to waking consciousness because it is able to connect different areas and functions of the brain. In contemporary theories of dreaming (Hartmann, 2010), there is general agreement that dreams reflect the efforts of an individual to adapt to reality: The dream is

> an unconscious attempt to find a solution to an emotionally relevant concern. In dreams people think about their main concerns, particularly those concerns that they have been unable to solve by conscious thought alone and try to develop and test plans and policies for dealing with them.
> (Gazzillo et al., 2020, p. 187)

The models of dream functions and meanings based on empirical dream research

> assume that (a) dreams are orderly and not random experiences; (b) dreams are meaningful, that is, the content of dreams is overtly or covertly related to the waking life of the dreamers; and (c) dreams play some important psychological function.
> (ibid. p. 187)

In general, research on the content of dreams found that it is closely and systematically correlated to various dimensions of the waking life of the dreamer (Zadra & Domhoff, 2010), this being the reason why the most prominent theory in dream research today is the so-called continuity hypothesis (Schredl et al., 2022), which states that there is no fundamental difference between waking state and dream mentation. Iftikhar et al. (2020) point out that dreams have a significant connection with waking life activities like decision making, personality traits and stressful events and have an impact on the way of dealing with psychological problems. Object representations in dreams were strong predictors of therapists' judgments of their patients' levels of object representations in waking life (Eudell-Simmons & Hilsenroth, 2005). Bódizs et al. (2008) investigated dreams from 5009 subjects, and the results indicate that the emotional content of dreaming is related to self-assessment of health status, number of days absent due to illness and subjective well-being. Negative feelings during dreaming correlate with illness; positive with health. The results of these studies demonstrate the potential of dreams to provide valuable clinical information to therapists, also because dream reports are less biased by social and communicational expectations. It was even demonstrated that the first dream presented in an analytic therapy ("initial dream") reflects themes of key importance for the later therapy (Bradlow & Bender, 1997; Kramer, 2015).

> Dreaming is an orderly event that is structured and reflects important psychological differences, responds to immediate emotional concerns, and is related to the waking preoccupations of the dreamer. [...] The psychodynamic theme from a dream translation of the first dream reported can predict the core psychodynamic theme to be found in therapy.
>
> (Kramer, 2015, p. 8)

Hall and Van de Castle (1966), who developed the above-mentioned coding system for the content of dreams, argued that it is possible to draw a personality profile based only on the dreams of a person. Furthermore, there is substantial continuity in the themes in dreams of a person over a long period of time (Levin, 1990), but the themes in the dreams change when a person goes through psychotherapy (Cart-wright, 1977). Warner (1983), in a study titled "Can psychoanalytic treatment change dreams", provides evidence and a number of detailed examples of how the treatment improved health, and namely the self-soothing capacity of analysands, which clearly showed in parallel changes in their dreams. Greenberg and Pearlman (1978) compared the content of dreams of subjects undergoing psycho-analytic treatment with verbatim minutes from the previous and the subsequent therapy session and found a clear correspondence. Palombo (1982) was able to show that in dreams analysands reworked contents from the directly preceding analytic session that could be recognized as such without decoding. Popp et al. (1990) compared dream reports and reports in the therapy session with an interpretive research methodology known as the Core Conflictual Relationship Theme. Here not only similarities of content but even correspondences in the unconscious underlying relational conflict patterns were ascertained. Extensive empirical studies have also been carried out by the psychoanalysts Kramer and Glucksman (2015). First, they were able to show that the content of dreams is influenced by the dreamer's sex, age and socio-economic level, as well as by psychic disorders, especially depression and schizophrenia. A very clear connection could be made between the dreamer's emotionally significant experiences and the themes that arose in the dreams. In sleep laboratory studies, they were also able to show that in the dreams of one night one prominent emotional theme was repeatedly reworked and that this dream content even over 20 nights did not fundamentally change. They explicitly summarize: The emotional intensity of the experience determines its effect on the dream. This effect is so strong that independent evaluators can identify the per-son's immediate and long-term significant themes from dreams alone.

Dreams can not only provide diagnostic information about a patient, but also there is evidence that dream content can reflect changes or improvement of a patient throughout the psychother-apeutic process. A number of case studies (Eudell-Simmons & Hilsenroth, 2005) found significant changes in dream content over the course of therapy, e.g. that pleasant emotional content of dreams increased in conjunction with positive clinical change. Those changes in dreams reflected the clinical improvement by more adaptive and integrated actions of dealing with problems and conflicts. The overall pattern of patients' dreams throughout the therapeutic process corresponded to progressive changes in dynamics and personality structure, in self-representation, defenses, interpersonal relationships, transference reactions and resolution of core conflicts. Ellis (2016) investigated qualitative changes in nightmares from five patients suffering from PTSD after successful trauma-oriented treatment. After the trauma-oriented treatment, the identity of the dream aggressor changed from known to unknown or vice versa, the dream ego actions progressed from passive to active responses (shifting from freeze to flight to fight, seeking help or taking action) and settings changed from original trauma settings to including more elements from current life.

Patients who improved over the course of psychotherapy compared to non-improved patients showed significant changes in the manifest dream content in contrast to the non-improved patients with only little change in the dream content (Eudell-Simmons & Hilsenroth, 2005). In successful treatments, the initial dreams with masochistic or self-punitive themes changed to later dreams with greater self-soothing capability and more self-satisfying themes. Depressed patients who showed little clinical improvement did not experience a change in masochistic themes in their dreams.

It is now well established that working with dreams in psychotherapy contributes significantly to improvement over the course of therapy compared to a group in which dreams were not addressed (Fiss, 1979; Hill, 1996, 2004; Glucksman & Kramer, 2011). Eudell-Simmons and Hilsenroth (2005) discuss

> four contributions of dreams to psychotherapy [...] as being particularly relevant for clinicians in applied practice to (I) facilitate the therapeutic process, (II) facilitate patient insight and self-awareness, (III) provide clinically relevant and valuable information to therapists and (IV) provide a measure of therapeutic change.
>
> (p. 260)

Chapter 10

Psychoanalytic clinical dream research

Independently of empirical dream research, there were also empirical studies on dreams and their significance in psychotherapy very early on in psychoanalysis itself. In contrast to the empirical dream research described above, however, this clinical dream research is less basic research and more an investigation of the significance of dreams in the context of psychotherapeutic treatment and the effects of therapeutic work with dreams on the progress of psychotherapy.

The comprehensive study of dreams begins with Freud's detailed analysis of the Irma dream, in which he uses a concrete dream example to "demonstrate the possibilities and imponderables of such an undertaking" (Fischmann, Leuzinger-Bohleber & Kächele, 2012, p. 834), which can be seen as the starting point of a new line of research. However, this interpretative approach in psychoanalytic research was also criticized early on by psychoanalysts themselves:

> Without doubt, it seems to me, a considerable and not unjustified part of the doubt about dream analysis as a science stems from the fact that almost without exception it begins with an interpretation of content that allows great subjective leeway with relatively limited objective verification possibilities.
>
> (Bash, 1988, p. 145)

An example for this is the study conducted by Robbins and Tanck (1980), who investigated Freudian concepts of sexual symbolism

DOI: 10.4324/9781003492078-11

in dreams. They had 87 unmarried college students keep a dream diary for nine days. The recorded dreams were analyzed using specially developed coding lists for sexual symbols. In addition, questionnaires were used to record the subjects' general sexual satisfaction and dating frequency. In accordance with the authors' hypotheses, it was shown that the group that had a satisfying sex life had significantly fewer sexual symbols in their dreams than the group that was dissatisfied and had few to no dates. This was interpreted as a confirmation of Freud's wish fulfillment theory. The results must be qualified by the fact that the coding of dream symbols as sexual was based entirely on classical Freudian concepts. Furthermore, the result could just as well be explained by Jung's compensation theory.

A number of Freudian authors have investigated Freud's assumptions about dreams in their own empirical studies but have also found findings of general significance for the understanding of dreams and dream interpretation. Empirical studies in psychoanalysis began with Alexander (1925), who was also the first to take a systematic look at dream series. Further earlier studies were carried out by French (1954).

The investigation of dream series and dream processes in psychotherapy

Recent psychoanalytic research on dreams usually examines coherent dream series of a dreamer or patient over the course of psychotherapy. However, looking at the dream in series was not always a matter of course, not even within psychoanalysis. Deserno and Kächele (2013) argue:

> Roughly speaking, one can illustrate almost anything one wants to show with a single dream, depending on the perspective taken. In contrast, the presentation of a dream series determines the extent to which the understanding of the narrated dreams changes and possibly, as a consequence, the narrated dreams themselves and possibly also the symptoms, etc.
>
> (p. 235; transl. C.R.)

It is therefore recommended here to examine dream series instead of individual dreams, as these provide more valid results.

The first systematic analysis of dream series in a scientific sense was carried out by Alexander in 1925 in his study "Dream pairs and dream series", in which the repetition of dream content was discussed for the first time (Fischmann et al., 2012). Alexander (1925) used clinical cases to show that he was able to add a dynamic component to Freud's (1900) observation that successive dreams (often on the same night or in successive therapy sessions) with the same latent dream content can be interpreted with increasing clarity. He found that in paired dreams, the first dream was often the precondition for the second dream. The wish fulfillment only seemed greater through the second dream, and the dream content became more manifest.

Jung also examined entire dream series in his famous dream seminars (Jung, 2001) and assumed that dreams continue over a longer period of time until the consciousness has grasped and processed the dream content in order to then make room for new dreams. He saw the inner sequence of meaning as radially arranged around a core of meaning.

From then on, research was no longer concerned with singular dreams but with the recurrence of themes in dreams, analysis and the question of why dream work "must always struggle with the same theme" (ibid., p. 835). In the introduction to his early work on dream research, French (1954) already points out that every dream also has a logical structure and that the logical structures of different dreams of the same person are linked to each other, so that all these dreams of one person are part of a single communication structure. He was able to prove that the affective range in the dream series is narrower at the beginning of a therapy and becomes wider and wider as the therapy progresses. Among the early studies on dream series, Deserno and Kächele (2013) also mention a study by Alexander Mitscherlich from 1947, in which he examined complete dream series and even provided some of these in the appendix – for example, a complete list of 103 dreams of an analysand (which is investigated below).

Mentzos (1995) was also able to show that with regard to dream functions, the sequence of dreams is not random and that an inner connection can be identified analogous to a dramaturgical staging. Dream functions here refer to self-presentation in the sense of playing through self-designs in different phases of life and object-relationship designs, living through conflicts from different perspectives and demonstrating different attempts at solutions.

It should be noted that a distinction must be made between the dreamed, the remembered and the narrated dream (Moser & von Zeppelin, 1996). The dream that is told in the psychotherapy session does not have to be identical to the dream at night, as a transformation is already carried out during recollection and translation into language. Visual material is already translated into language during the process of remembering and is therefore subject to transformation. If the dream is then narrated or written down, this narrative is dependent on situational factors such as the interest of the listener and their reaction to the narrative. Depending on various factors, e.g. the listener's style of questioning, some details are remembered and others are not. In addition, many dreams are not remembered at all, and even the dreams that are remembered are largely not recounted. The only link between waking life and the dream is the memory of the dream and the linguistic reproduction of the dream. In this way, the focus is expanded, as it were, from the dreaming individual to an interaction (Moser & von Zeppelin, 1996) – even if it is an interaction of the dreamer with himself, when he remembers the dream and sets about writing it down, thus narrating the dream to himself. Only at the moment in which the dream undergoes a transformation in the sense of memory and verbalization does it become a communicative object and thus also accessible to scientific research. Since the dream memory does not correspond to the dream dreamed during sleep, it could be said on the one hand that the actual phenomenon of the dreamed dream is fundamentally inaccessible to scientific research, at least as far as its meaning is concerned. On the other hand, psychoanalytic dream researchers assume that the dream narrative can be admitted as an object of research and understand it as an expression of the dream process that develops during waking daytime experience (Hamburger, 1999). However, it is assumed that there is at least a structural identity between the dreamed and remembered or reproduced dream (Moser & von Zep-pelin, 1996). Of particular interest in recent psychoanalytic work is the representation of the dream and its modeling by the narrator. The dream is thus treated as a story or narrative. Moreover, as every psy-choanalyst knows, the narration of a dream is dependent on situational factors such as the transference relationship, defense phenomena, the current mood, etc. For this reason, the communication of a dream must nowadays always be regarded as a communication within the transference relationship. Furthermore, it is likely that only a fraction of the dreams dreamed are remembered, and only a fraction of these are recounted. A certain objectification can be achieved through the practice in Jungian analysis of making the patient keep a dream diary in which he always enters all remembered dreams as quickly as possible. It must therefore be assumed that the narrated dream is a product of a further developing dream process, although a structural identity of the dreamed dream with the remembered and narrated dream can be assumed (Moser & von Zeppelin, 1996). Therefore, in more recent conceptions, the dream is regarded as a narrative. In discourse analytic studies it was also demonstrated in detail how the meaning of a dream is jointly constructed in the dialogue of analyst and analysand (Peräkylä & Bergmann, 2020).

In 1968, Enke, Ohlmeier and Nast carried out a formal affect and relationship analysis of dream series of patients with psychosomatic illnesses, for which psychotherapeutic sessions were recorded on tape for the first time. This research on systematic dream corpora was subsequently continued at the University of Ulm in Germany. A number of outstanding studies within German psychoanalytic dream research are based on recordings of psychoanalytic treatments as part of the Ulm Textbank, which taped psychoanalytic treatments, transcribed the sessions and offered these for research (see overview in Fischmann et al., 2012; an example is the case Amalia X described below). Leuzinger-Bohleber (1989) initially developed a procedure for the investigation of dreams based on the diary of an analysand. She then used the method developed in this way to analyze the first and last 100 analysis hours of completely audio-recorded psychoanalytic treatments. Based on the coding system according to Moser and von Zeppelin (1996), she then examined 112 dreams from five long-term psychoanalytic therapies – in each case dreams from the first and last 100 sessions. It was shown that the instrument can depict individually different affect patterns. They also found that the dreams at the end of the therapy differed from those at the beginning in the case of positive treatment courses, which was not the case in unsuccessful therapy, where there were no such changes. Furthermore, the spectrum of affects in the manifest dream content (e.g. motifs of surprise, joy, pride, triumph, sadness, distancing) was expanded in successful therapy. Furthermore, anxiety dreams occurred less frequently than at the beginning of the treatment. There were more successful than unsuccessful solutions to problems, and the dream ego was more active and less often in the observer position. In addition, as the studies by Hall and Van de Castle (1966) had already shown, there were fewer animal representations and more people and more mature object relationships. Detailed individual observation of one of the dream series showed that the quality of the relationships changed, became friendlier and more caring, that self-related negative emotions in dreams decreased significantly and that the ability to successfully solve problems became more and more prevalent over the course of the dream series. Object-related negative emotions, on the other hand, showed stable variability around a mean value.

Leuzinger-Bohleber et al. were also able to find corresponding changes in the LAC depression studies (long-term analytic vs. cognitive-behavioral treatment of chronic depression; Fischmann et al., 2012). They were able to prove empirically

> that successful psychoanalyses – compared to less successful psychoanalyses – are characterized, among other things, by the fact that the dream atmosphere changes positively, more successful than unsuccessful problem solutions take place, the affective spectrum changes (among other things, nightmares no longer predominate as at the beginning), the dreamer hardly appears in an observer perspective, but more helping

persons appear in the dream plot [...] In addition, we expect, especially in severely traumatized patients, that the destruction of the inner structures is evident in the manifest dreams at the beginning of the treatments.

(Fischmann & Leuzinger-Bohleber, 2018, p. 171)

Leuzinger-Bohleber (2013) formulates the following thesis based on these results:

> Dreams are both an expression of drive (in the sense of endogenous stimulation stemming from internal sources) and of current and past object relations. The dream ego is simultaneously pleasure-seeking and object-seeking and tries out problem solutions for current events in connection with central conflictual complexes. Therefore, the solutions to problems in dreams can contain indications of turning points in psychoanalytic treatment and therapeutic changes.
>
> (p. 267)

Kächele also found similar results in various studies (see overview in Kächele, 2012).

Fischmann et al. (2012) provide an overview of the diverse methodological approaches to dreams in current psychoanalytic dream research. Using an example from the LAC depression study, the authors show the changes in the patient's dreams in the course of analytic treatment. These consist above all of a more active attitude of the dream ego, which no longer sees itself passively flooded by unbearable affects, as well as better relationship patterns of the subject in the dream. In particular, the subject in the dream no longer assumes a distanced observer position but is actively involved in the dream events and endeavors to solve problems, as with Leuzinger-Bohleber (1989).

Döll-Hentschker (2008) also examined 142 dreams from five psychoanalyses using the coding model of Moser and von Zeppelin (1996) and came to the conclusion that the validity of the dream coding could be confirmed. The following hypotheses were confirmed:

1   Individually different patterns of affect regulation were found in the individual cases.
2   Intra-individual differences were found between the beginning and end of treatment when the course of treatment was positive.
3   There were individually different developments for these intraindividual changes.
4   Minor or negative changes were found if the course of treatment was unsuccessful.
5   There were also changes that were comprehensible and justifiable in terms of the flexibilization of affect regulation.
6   The clinical assessments already available were consistent with these empirical results.

Recently, Kempe, Köpp and Wittmann (2024), have demonstrated for patients with personality disorders that decreasing impairment of personality functioning in the course of therapy is associated with increases in the capacity for affect regulation in dreams.

Deserno and Kächele (2013) summarize these findings in the following hypothesis: The organization of the individual dream depends in each case on the solutions found in the preceding dreams. However, the decisive transformative factor here is the relationship between patient and analyst. In particular, how they succeed in using the solution offered by the dream for the local conflicts in the transference.

The above-mentioned results of psychoanalytic research on therapeutic work with dreams show that working with dreams in therapy has both diagnostic and therapeutic relevance. This research also proves that dreams can be used to make the dreamer's current psychodynamics and potential for change and processes of change visible during therapy.

Exemplary presentation of psychoanalytic clinical dream research on the case of Amalia X

In a videotaped psychoanalytic treatment from the Ulm Text-bank, the treatment of Amalia X, the best-studied individual case in the history of psychotherapy research, 96 dream reports were identified and examined from various perspectives

(Mergenthaler et al., 2006). This psychoanalytic therapy of 531 sessions was recorded in full on video/audio as part of the Ulm Textbank and then transcribed in order to make it available to researchers for psychotherapy research (Kächele, Leuzinger-Bohleber, Buchheim & Thomä, 2006). This analysis is considered exemplary and successful; it has been verified by standardized measurement instruments and used as a model case in various textbooks on psychoanalytic therapy. It has also been analyzed in a whole series of scientific studies.

The patient Amalie sought psychotherapy in the 1970s at the age of 35 for depressive moods and low self-esteem. The psychoanalysis was successful. In addition to the assessment by the treating psychotherapist, this was also verified by the use of standardized measurement instruments, in this case the Freiburg Personality Inventory and the Giessen Test (Kächele et al., 2006).

The patient's self-esteem disorder and the associated depression are closely linked to a hereditary disorder known as hirsutism – male pattern hair growth – which Amalie has suffered from all over her body since puberty. Naturally, the development of a female identity was considerably impaired as a result. The feeling of being stigmatized combined with obsessive-compulsive and other neurotic symptoms and anxieties to create a vicious circle in which she became increasingly insecure about entering into social relationships and, in particular, heterosexual partnerships. During her childhood and adolescence, her father was often absent due to his work, which made the patient feel that she was becoming a substitute partner for her mother. She was successful in school and education and completed a degree to become a secondary school teacher. Until the first analysis session, she had not had any sexual contact. At the beginning of therapy, she was diagnosed with dysthymia (ICD-10 F34.1).

According to the results of the standardized measurement instruments, she was less burdened by psychosomatic symptoms at the end of therapy, was generally happier, had better self-esteem, was more extraverted and well socially integrated.

A total of 96 dreams were discussed as part of this psychoanalysis, and a number of scientific studies are also available on these (Levy, Ablon, Ackerman, Thomä & Kächele, 2012; Boothe, 2006, 2018; Kächele, Eberhardt & Leuzinger-Bohleber, 1999; Merkle, 1987; Mathys, 2001). In a study by Merkle (1987), dreams from the beginning and end of therapy were compared with each other. Systematic changes were found to the effect that better relationships appeared in the dreams at the end of therapy; these were friendlier and gentler than in the early dreams. In addition, the emotional atmosphere in the dreams was friendlier, and problems could be solved better. The results showed that the percentage of successful problem-solving strategies in the dreams increased towards the end of the therapy, while the unsuccessful strategies decreased. The emotional atmosphere in the dreams also changed towards the end of the treatment, with negative emotions about the dream ego itself decreasing. The author concluded that the changes in the course of the treatments were clearly reflected in the change in the structure of the dreams (Kächele, 2012).

Boothe (2018) reports on the results of a narrative analysis of dreams from different phases of therapy in comparison with the patient's interactive self-positioning in the therapeutic interview: It was found that the patient's self-awareness and autonomy in the self-positioning in the dreams corresponded with those from the transcripts of the therapeutic sessions. In addition, when analyzing the dreams from the final phase of therapy, it was noticeable that the dream ego had gained independence and self-confidence in relation to the other figures and felt comfortable in its autonomy.

This change in the dreams parallels the changes in the patient's well-being over the course of the therapy: There was a significant improvement in her self-esteem. The patient's subjective suffering also decreased continuously over the course of the analysis. The patient's preoccupation with her own limitations and insecurities receded, and instead she began to actively influence her environment and pursue her plans (Kächele et al., 2006).

The 96 dreams in the case of Amalie X were also examined using the research method of structural dream analysis described below, which confirmed the results described above. In addition, it yielded further interesting findings that make it possible to comment on the validity of the various psychoanalytic dream theories.

Fundamental problems of the scientific investigation of the content of dreams

As shown above, there is a whole range of approaches both within psychoanalysis and outside of it in empirical dream research to scientifically investigate the content of dreams and thereby establish links to the dreamer's waking life or to the course of psychotherapy. Fonagy et al. (2012) provide an overview of the relevant psychoanalytic clinical dream research.

The problem with psychoanalytic research on dreams is often that certain elements of the theoretical view of dreams, whether by Freud or others, are taken for granted and can therefore no longer be falsified in the course of research. For example, the coding system of Moser and von Zeppelin (1991, 1996) implicitly assumes that the dream has the function of protecting sleep and on this basis examines changing positions of elements in the dream in relation to each other, whereby the dream fulfills this function. The problem here is that "the search for internal validity may be circular. Meaning collected according to a method of meaning cannot be used to validate the method" (Marcus, 2003, p. 369).

On the other hand, there are coding systems, such as the famous system of Hall and Nordby (1972), which simply count the occurrence of certain symbols or elements in dreams. Typical dreams or dream motifs reported in this classification include aggression, predators, flying, traps, being chased by hostile strangers, landscapes, misfortune, sex, getting married and having children, trials, traveling, swimming or being in water, watching fires, and being held captive in an underground place. The problem with this kind of classification is that these typical dream motifs describe very different entities – from objects and living beings to patterns of action and story structures. There is no theoretical model behind such a classification that could link the dream motifs to a meaning for the dreamer. Therefore, such systems are not able to capture the meaning of dreams. This has already been criticized by Stevens (1995), who gives the following example:

> Simple content analyses reveal that agonistic dreams are more common among males of all ages and hedonic dreams more

common among females, but both types of dreams occur in both sexes. A more significant variable than gender in determining the relative incidence of such dreams is the kind of family the individual grew up in.

(p. 249)

A famous precursor of such lists of typical dreams/dream motifs comes from Freud himself: In his *Interpretation of Dreams* (1900), he describes typical dreams or dream motifs, including embarrassment, testing, being hunted, flying and falling, and others. A more recent attempt to determine typical dream motifs empirically comes from the Italian research group led by Maggiolini, Morelli, Falotico and Montali (2016), which works with the manualized "Typical Dream Questionnaire" method. Previous research using this method identified being chased (81.5%), sexual experiences (76.5%), falling (63.8%) and school context (67.1%) as the most common dream motives, which interestingly are consistent across countries as diverse as Canada, USA, Japan, Germany and China. The research group's current study identifies five clusters of dreams: Fear and escape, school, competition and sports, attack and entrapment, and spatial disorientation.

There have already been various attempts to avoid overloading the research methodology with theoretical assumptions and still arrive at an interpretation of the meaning of the dream through simple counting.

Morgenthaler (1992) describes an approach to dream analysis that also incorporates the phenomenological-daseinsanalytical perspective. This demands that nothing more be sought behind the phenomena and that all dream theories be abandoned. Here, different theoretical assumptions, as well as the procedures derived from them in dream analysis, are integrated, and the analysis of the dream content is understood as a hermeneutic process. The dream ego is thus understood as an acting ego, and from this it is concluded that an examination of the dream must concentrate on the action structure of the dream.

Morgenthaler criticizes current scientific approaches for focusing too much on the symbolic quality of the individual dream parts and for losing sight of the plot line. The author suggests understanding dreams as imaginary actions and examining them in the same way as everyday actions can be explored. Everyday actions can be investigated by asking about goals, the subject of the action, the form of the action, alternative actions, the hierarchical organization, the success of the action and the emotions accompanying the action. By analogy, Morgenthaler explores the dream. Although no systematic procedure is described here, there is a broadening of perspective in relation to dream analysis, namely by also looking at the action structure of the dream.

Hamburger (2006) understands the dream as a narrative and, based on psychoanalytical considerations, examines the dream narrative from the point of view of its temporal structure. The dream narrative situates the arrangement of an action sequence in time, whereby the author focuses on the investigation of how the presented temporal structures affect the accompanying affects of the analyst. One focus of the investigation is therefore on the interactive aspect of the dream narrative.

It is interesting to note that the author takes a look at the plot and structural elements of the narratives when analyzing the dream narratives. Furthermore, he explores the dramaturgy of the narrative by drawing on Boothe's (2002) methodological approach to narrative analysis, which also provides essential impulses for the structural dream analysis presented below. Although Hamburger's research interest in the cited work has a different focus, it is clear that attempts have already been made to treat dreams as narratives and to apply the methodology of text-analytical procedures to dreams in a fruitful way.

A structuralist approach

The following questions are of particular interest for clinical dream research:

- Is the content of dreams linked to the psychological situation (the inner world) of the dreamer and in particular to psychological problems or disorders, and if so, how in detail?

- If therapeutic change takes place in the context of psychotherapy, is there a parallel in the content of dreams?
- How can we then understand the function of dreams? Do
  dreams in this sense rather give a picture of the overall situation of the psyche including unconscious aspects (Jung) or
  must the dream content rather be seen as a distortion of the
  latent (unconscious) meaning and as fulfilling the function of
  wish fulfillment (Freud)?

If one assumes Jung's perspective and that of other contemporary
theories that the dream is a representation of the dreamer's current
psychological situation (which is rather supported by the empirical
dream research described above), then the link between dream
content and the dreamer's psychological problems or situation
would be reflected above all in the relationship between the dream
ego and other figures in the dream – in the sense of the extent of
the dream ego's activity (agency) and its ability to act, exercise
willpower and deal with and overcome problems in the dream.

Fischmann and Leuzinger-Bohleber (2018), even if their
approach is based more on a Freudian model of the dream, formulate a very similar idea based on the model already presented
by Moser and von Zeppelin:

> According to this, it can be assumed that a dream complex
> stems from one or more complexes stored in long-term
> memory which have found their roots in conflictual and/or
> traumatic experiences and in introjects usually associated with
> them. These conflictual or traumatic dream complexes can
> easily be triggered by stimuli from the outside world that are
> structurally similar to the situations of the complexes stored
> in memory. The desired solution to the complex is determined
> by the need for security and the desire to participate in social
> life or engage in relationships.
>
> (1996, p. 169, transl. C.R.)

The idea that, from a psychoanalytic perspective, the relationship
of the dream ego to the other elements in the dream is particularly
interesting and that the activity of the dream ego and its success

reflects what is referred to in psychoanalysis as ego strength (or structural integration or maturity) is supported by further concepts from empirical dream research. The advantages of such a structuralist approach, in which the focus is not on individual elements of the dream, but rather on the relationship of elements in the dream to each other (here: the dream ego to the other elements in the dream), are, for example:

- The result of such research would no longer be disparate elements based on a count, but rather structural patterns and the question of how these change over a series of dreams.
- Such a method would not, as already shown above and as is often the case with other research methods, contain an overload of theoretical concepts, which can then no longer be verified as such.

Structural Dream Analysis

In the method Structural Dream Analysis (hereafter, SDA) (Roesler, 2018b), the inclusion of any theoretical assumptions about the dream was minimized. SDA assumes that the meaning of dreams is not so much transmitted by the elements or symbols in the dream but more by the relationship between elements in the dream (structure), especially the relationship of the dream ego to other elements in the dream and the extent of agency of the dream ego. This approach is more interested in identifying patterns than in coding elements, especially patterns of relationship of the dream ego to other figures and elements in the dream; e.g. whether the dream ego is in an active or passive position regarding the actions occurring in the dream, whether the dream ego is actively authoring what is happening in the dream or is subjected to other figures' actions. SDA sees the dream as a narrative which allows for the use of analytic tools developed in narratology (for more details, see Roesler, 2018a). In narratology, a narrative is defined as a development from a starting point, which is a problem that needs repair or solution, and how the protagonist deals with the problem and eventually solves it. Thus, a dream is a short story about how the protagonist, in most cases the dream ego, processes a problem. There are a number of approaches in dream research which have taken a similar viewpoint (Sparrow, 2020), e.g. the concept of active control of the dream ego over the happenings in the dream, or the measuring of the occurrence of problems within a dream (Schredl, 2018, p. 48). SDA is a qualitative, interpretive research method that attempts to formalize the process of interpretation of the dream in a way that the conclusions are independent from the interpreter (see below for reliability tests). The meaning conveyed by the dream is analyzed in a systematic series of interpretive steps for which a formalized manual is available (Roesler, 2018b).

The phases of research with SDA

In a first phase, in which the methodology was developed, a complex set of (narratological) methods of analysis was applied to well-documented single cases in an inductive (bottom-up) manner of qualitative analysis, i.e. the researchers attempted to identify typical, repetitive patterns characterizing the dream series of the case from the text alone, without carrying theoretical concepts into the material. The narratological methods treated the dreams as narrative texts and included:

Agency of the dream ego: based on Boothe's (2002) analysis of patient narratives and their development over the course of therapy, this method focuses on the role the narrator takes in the narrative in terms of activity vs. passivity and his/her relation to other protagonists in the narrative, as well as on different episodic models (e.g. continuity, climax, anticlimax) which describe the course the narrative takes.

Functional Analysis: (following Vladimir Propp's (1975) method of analyzing fairy tales) reducing the complexity of the dream into abstract patterns (e.g. the dream ego is threatened, flight, the dream ego confronts the threat etc.).

A detailed description of the methodology of this first phase of SDA and its application to a case example can be found in Roesler (2018b). The material was provided by practicing therapists and consisted of a series of dreams ideally covering the whole of the process of psychotherapy; diagnostic information: Biography, symptoms, psychopathology, ICD diagnoses, unconscious conflicts/ complexes and a model of the psychodynamics; and a report by the therapist of the course of therapy, the major themes and the results in terms of improvement. In this first phase, 15 well-documented cases with a total of 206 dreams were thoroughly investigated with this extensive, single case analysis form of SDA (for details see Roesler, 2018b).

In a second phase, with these 15 cases analyzed as a basis, a cross-case analysis was conducted which aimed at identifying interindividually typical patterns of dreams; for these means, a qualitative analysis following the Grounded Theory methodology (Glaser & Strauss, 2009) was conducted, aiming at identifying categories which were typical for a number of cases in the sample and forming a theoretical model. These patterns were connected with the initial level of psychopathology of the patients as well as with the course of therapy and improvements gained, and the crucial explanatory variable was found to be the agency of the dream ego. As a result of this phase, a typology of dream patterns was created (see Table 10.1) as well as a theoretical model of the relations between dreams/dream patterns, initial psychopathology and the course of psychotherapy (for details, see Roesler, 2018b). With this typology it was possible to categorize more than 90% of the dreams in the study.

The dream patterns represent the general idea of SDA that the dream is a micronarrative in which a problem is presented which the dream ego has to struggle with, i.e. the ego is confronted with a requirement, has to cope with a challenge or attempts to fulfill a plan or task. The agency of the dream ego rises continually, starting from pattern 1 (no ego present at all); in patterns 2 and 3, the dream ego is present but under pressure from other forces in the dream, i.e. the initiative is not with the ego but it is subjected to their power and control; in patterns 4 and 5, the ego has taken over the initiative and attempts to follow a personal plan; in pattern 5 this focuses on creating satisfying relationships with others (including sexual contact); finally, in pattern 6, the dream ego gains full autonomy from others and can move freely. The same movement towards more agency of the dream ego applies to each of the patterns, e.g. inside pattern 2 there is a movement from

Table 10.1 Typology of dream types/patterns

Type 1: No dream ego present
The dream ego does not participate in the plot (dreamer observes a scene as if watching a movie)

Type 2: The dream ego is threatened
The dream ego is threatened or pursued by a threatening figure

2.1 The dream ego is completely destroyed, damaged, dismembered, severely wounded or even killed

2.2 The dream ego is overwhelmed, i.e. completely powerless, no coping strategy

2.3 The dream ego flees from the threat

2.4 The dream ego defends itself, i.e. has a strategy, but the threat remains

2.5 The dream ego successfully defends itself against the threat (threat transforms to non-dangerous)

Type 3: The dream ego is confronted with a performance requirement
The dream ego encounters a performance requirement (e.g. an examination) set by other characters in the dream; find something (which was previously lost), give something to someone, etc.

3.1 The dream ego fails (e.g. fails a test); is subjected to the control of others, against its will, cannot do anything about it

3.2 The dream ego is prepared but encounters obstacles. The task is ultimately not solved

3.3 The dream ego is subjected to the requirement but successfully copes with it through its own activity

Type 4: Mobility dream
The dream ego is on the way somewhere (specified or unclear destination): It follows its own initiative, tries to implement its own intentions or plans

4.1 The dream ego is locked up in a room, trying to find its way out or to break out but failing.

4.2 The dream ego wants to move, e.g. travel, but has no means, e.g. misses the train.

4.3 The dream ego moves successfully but encounters obstacles and the process cannot be continued.

4.4 The dream ego is in motion, encounters obstacles and the desired destination is not reached.

4.5 The dream ego manages to move successfully and reaches the desired destination.

Type 5: Social interaction
The dream ego is trying to communicate with someone, to create a satisfying encounter (includes sexuality).

5.1 The dream ego wants to get in contact with others but is ignored by the others.

5.2 The dream ego comes into contact with others but encounters obstacles; all in all, the attempt to establish a desired contact fails.

5.3 The dream ego is successful in establishing the desired contact.

Type 6: Autonomy dream
The dream ego establishes or defends its autonomy.

6.1 The dream ego is flooded by the affection of others.

6.2 The dream ego is aggressive towards others (even kills them), which expresses the will of the dream ego to be separate and independent from others.

6.3 The dream ego is on its own and content.

6.4 The dream ego helps others (has so many resources left that it can provide them to the others, but it is the initiative of the dream ego)

---

pattern 2.1 with a completely powerless dream ego to 2.5 in which the dream ego successfully overcomes the threat.

The Theoretical Model: The dream patterns can be interpreted psychologically as an expression of the capacity of the dreamer's ego, on different levels, to regulate or cope with emotions, motivations and complexes. The extent of agency of the dream ego is equivalent to what psychoanalysis calls ego strength or maturity of the personality, i.e. the degree of integration of ego and other parts of the psyche into the whole of the personality and the capacity of ego functioning (Blanck & Blanck, 1974).

In those cases in which psychotherapy was successful, such that there was an improvement in symptoms, psychological well-being, regulation of emotion and, from a psychoanalytic point of view, a gain in ego strength (structural integration of the personality), a typical pattern of transformation was found in the structure of the dreams (see Figure 10.1). Typically the first phase of the psychotherapeutic process was dominated by a repetitive pattern in the dreams, which showed a weak dream ego incapable of solving the problem presented in the dream: e.g. the dream ego is

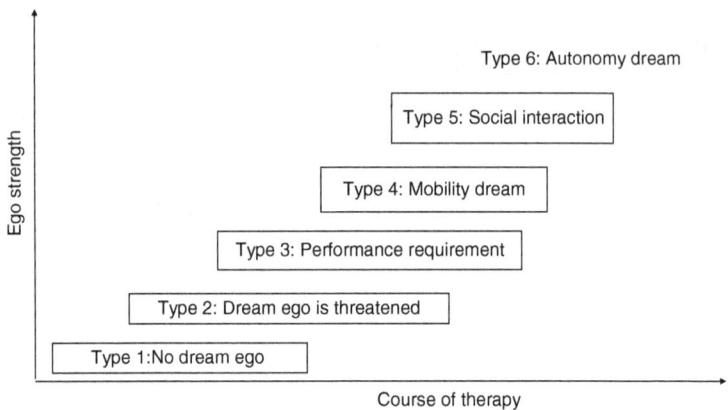

Figure 10.1 Dream patterns, ego strength and course of therapy

threatened and typically has no strategy to cope with the threat, and therefore flees or attempts to hide; in pattern 3, the dream ego has to fulfill a task (e.g. an examination) but typically fails, is not prepared, is too late etc.; in mobility dreams (pattern 4), the dream ego typically fails to reach the desired aim, is on the wrong bus or train or has no ticket etc. If psychotherapy is successful, the typical patterns change into more successful activities of the dream ego: e.g. it confronts threatening figures, fights actively and successfully overcomes the threat, fulfills the tasks (e.g. passes an exam) or succeeds in reaching the desired aim and controls the means of transportation. In general, there is a movement from lower patterns (1, 2 and 3) dominating the first half of the dream series, in which the dream ego is subjected to others' initiative or even threatened, towards patterns 4, 5 and 6 in the second half of the dream series, in which the dream ego gains more and more agency and solves the problem in the dream successfully, e.g. is more and more capable of creating satisfying interactions with others, including sexual encounters, or even makes itself contently independent from others. This transformation is interpreted from a psychodynamic perspective as speaking to the fact that an initially weak ego structure which fails to regulate and integrate threatening emotions, impulses and complexes gains in ego strength over the course of the therapy and more and more succeeds in coping with initially suppressed or split off parts of the psyche and integrates these into constructive interactions with others. These gains are reflected in real life by the person becoming more and more capable of executing willpower, conducting their plans, regulating emotions and expressing their needs in social interactions. This follows the model of personality integration as formulated by Operationalized Psychodynamic Diagnostics (OPD) Task Force (2008). In addition to this model of transformation, there is a close connection between the initial level of ego strength/structural integration of the personality at the start of therapy on the one side, and the level of dominating pattern in the first half of the dream series on the other, in the sense that the scale of levels of ego strength/personality integration is reflected in the scale of dream patterns; e.g. patients whose dreams are shaped mainly by the threat–escape pattern (2) usually struggle with structural problems around an unstable ego and personality, whereas patients with dreams of mobility (pattern 4) and interpersonal relationships (pattern 5) seem to have more integrated personalities and higher ego strength and are preoccupied with more neurotic and interpersonal problems.

Symbolization

Beyond that, the relationship between the dream ego and threatening figures and the reaction of the dream ego to the threat is imaging the relationship between actual ego strength and unintegrated or conflicted parts of the psyche (complexes), unconscious and repressed needs and motivations. The special form the threatening figure takes in the dream – especially if the dream pattern is repetitive – can be seen as symbolizing the psychological problem, the complex or repressed impulse with which the dreamer is struggling. On the other hand, no support was found for the psychoanalytic assumption that there are typical or even fixed (e.g. archetypal) meanings for specific symbols. Example: In the case of a female dreamer, the dream ego is repeatedly threatened by snakes. In this case, the therapist diagnosed an unresolved conflict between a highly moralistic superego on the one hand and very lively but repressed sexual desires on the other.

The snake here can clearly be interpreted as a sexual, phallic symbol, which appears threatening to an ego under the pressure of the moralistic superego. In contrast to that, in the dreams of a young man the snake repeatedly has the role of a helper. In sum, symbols appearing repeatedly in dream series can often be interpreted as symbolic images for parts of the psyche, its impulses and complexes which are not yet integrated into the whole of personality and which therefore appear threatening to ego integrity. But the symbol has to be interpreted in the context of the personality and life course of the dreamer.

Research supporting the concept of dream ego agency

In a study on the dreams of persons with multiple personality disorder, Barrett (1996) was able to demonstrate that the split-off parts of their personalities appeared personified in their dreams. In a study of the dreams of pediatric oncology patients, Mendonça and Fortim (2018) found that the attitude of the dream ego illustrates the possibilities available to the ego: A passive dream ego reflects a lack of internal resources to face the condition in waking life, thus the dream reflects the current psychic situation of the individual's personality. Structural dream characteristics such as passive dream ego, threatening figures, lack of protective figures, or unpleasant or absent outcomes were predominant in the reports of children with cancer. "Fundamentally, these aspects indicate to us that the ego is failing to develop resources to deal with conflict, and its passive position is a major detriment to the development of its potentialities" (p. 75). Varvin et al. (2012) compared the dreams of 25 patients suffering from PTSD and 25 participants without PTSD. The dreams of PTSD patients showed patterns of frequent deterioration and destruction of the dream ego, threatening elements of the underlying dream complex that appeared undisguised, and passive behavior of the dream ego. In contrast, the dream ego in the control group was actively involved in the dream narrative, successfully solved problems of the dream complex more often, and the dream ends with success. The author found the same relationship as in SDA between psychopathology of the dreamer, dream structure and agency of the dream ego and

concludes that the dream provides information about the dreamer's ego strength. It is not only the aversive dream content that
makes a dream a nightmare, but the agency of the dream ego is
decisive. There is a parallel in narrative clinical research as it was
possible to link narrative agency with the extent of neuroticism/
psychopathology of patients as it showed in their narrations in the
context of psychotherapy, in so far as neurotic patients tend to
minimize or even deny their agency in autobiographical accounts
(Pfeifer, 2022). Schredl (2018) points to the close relationship
between mental disorders and the percentage of nightmares in the
dreams of a person, in the sense that nightmares are significantly
more frequent in disturbed persons, which confirms the idea that
in nightmares the failing capability of the dream ego is pictured to
deal with inner conflicts and problems: "The most common
nightmare themes are being chased, falling, and being late" (p.
147). According to Kalsched (1996), in the dreams of victims of
early trauma, the inner daimonic figure – representing the traumatic experience – actively attacks the dream ego. Sándor, Szakadát and Bódizs (2016) found that the presence and activity of the
dream ego in the dreams is strongly correlated with the extent of
effective coping and emotion regulation in the waking life of the
dreamer. Ellis (2016) found typical changes in the dreams of
patients with post-traumatic stress disorder after they had received
treatment: "Dream ego actions moved forward on a continuum
from freeze to flight to fight as dreamers began to find their voices,
seek help and/or take action" (p. 185). Experts who have developed therapeutic methods for the treatment of nightmares (e.g.
Imagery Rehearsal Therapy) emphasize that dream characters,
also threatening ones, might represent aspects of the dreamer's
personality, and thus active interaction with these dream characters is encouraged (Schredl, 2018). Calvin Hall (1966) found
that children dream more often of fearful animals than adults
(28% versus 7%), but the threatening animals appear increasingly
tame and controllable the older the child becomes. There is also a
correlation between lower social skills and more frequent animal
dreams in the same age group. Animals in dreams could symbolize impulses and affects that are not yet controllable and that are
experienced by the ego as a threat to its ability to control.

According to Foulkes (1982b), it takes up to thirteen years for the human capacity for dreaming to fully develop in parallel with cognitive and emotional development. In young children's dreams, there is usually no dream ego; this only emerges at the age of about seven.

A yet to be published Japanese study (Konakawa, in review) which investigated changes in the frequency of SDA dream patterns over the lifecycle found significant differences in so far as dream patterns 1 and 2 are more frequent in adolescents vs. dream patterns 3, 4 and 5 being more frequent in adults and the elderly, which is interpreted as a reflection of the yet instable ego in adolescence. This is confirmed by findings from Maggiolini et al. (2016), who found that dream content of "being chased" and "dream ego is threatened" (SDA: pattern 2) is more frequent in childhood and adolescence and decreases over the lifecycle, whereas "trying to do something again and again" and "arriving too late" (SDA: patterns 3 and 4) is more frequent in adults. They also argue, together with Nielsen et al. (2003) and Schredl (2018), for the universality of these dream themes across different cultures (for a detailed discussion of intercultural similarities and differences in dream themes, see Roesler et al., 2021). Concerning the connection between dreams and psychopathology, there is evidence that negative dream content (failure, helplessness, being chased) and nightmare frequency are related to neuroticism (Schredl et al., 2022; Carr et al., 2022). Güven and Bilim (2018) investigated a theoretical model which correlates defense mechanisms, dysfunctional attitudes and interpersonal relationship styles with disturbing dream themes, and could provide empirical support for their model. Dream themes such as anxiety, fear and frustration could be predicted by immature and neurotic defense mechanisms. Yu's (2013) study could demonstrate that superego functions such as defense mechanisms can predict negative dream content. In a study by Euler et al. (2016), the above-mentioned Moser and von Zeppelin coding system was used to analyze dreams of subjects who were also diagnosed by using the OPD system (see above). A correlation was found between the level of personality integration in the form of maturity of defense mechanisms and dream imagery, in the sense that subjects with integrated personality structure and more mature defense mechanisms had more lively and complex dreams. Very much in line with these findings, Kempe et al. (2024) found that decreasing impairment of affect regulation in patients over the course of therapy is paralleled by more involvement of the dream ego in dreams towards the end of therapy. In the same line, Warner (1983) found that in successful cases of psychoanalytic treatment there is a growing agency of the dream ego towards the end of therapy, more successful and satisfying dream narratives, and that the helplessness of the dream ego (called "masochistic motif") from the beginning phase of therapy vanishes.

An exemplary case study

The patient reported for psychotherapy after serving a prison sentence of several years for multiple counts of grievous bodily harm. On his release, he was recommended to undergo psychotherapy. In prison, the client had undergone a religious conversion and joined a fundamentalist Christian sect. He had managed to get his violent behavior under control, partly with the help of his sect's rigid morals, but he was still suffering from states of tension, restlessness and inner emptiness that were almost unbearable. The only way for him to combat these conditions was to consume pornographic videos, especially those in which women were subjected to violence. Then he would find inner peace, but afterwards he would feel burnt out. After a while, the inner restlessness would build up again. The patient had grown up in extremely difficult circumstances and experienced a very difficult childhood. His mother had a migrant background and his father had brought her to Germany from her home country in the Balkans. To this day, his mother has not learned to speak German properly and still behaves awkwardly in social situations, reports the client. She probably suffers from a mild mental disability. He was unable to respect his mother, and later even rejected her (e.g. he could not stand her body odor). The father had been an alcoholic and had always grabbed one of the children and beaten them up when he was drunk. On one occasion, the client's father choked him by the neck to such an extent that he thought he was going to die. The mother was unable to stop the father. As children, they had always tried to recognize what state the father was in so that they could hide if necessary. However, the father was very unpredictable. When the patient was about 14 or 15 years old, he began to fight back, which ended the domestic violence.

The father had a huge collection of pornographic videos hidden in a closet in the bedroom, which the client was extremely fascinated by. Apparently, the father had a sexual obsession and spent so much money on prostitutes that he almost ruined the family. The father had also been convicted of theft himself. As a teenager, the client was placed in a foster family by the youth welfare office due to the domestic circumstances, where the foster mother sexually abused him. As soon as possible, the client then lived alone and joined a group of delinquent youths with whom he committed numerous acts of violence, for which he was eventually convicted.

Due to these upbringing conditions and the violence experienced in the family, the client was severely traumatized, which explains the recurring depressive states. The earlier violent orientation can be understood as a desperate attempt to compensate for the inner emptiness and deep frustration caused by the experience of deprivation. What is impressive is his independent overcoming of this violent activity in prison and his orientation towards a strict moral structure that stabilizes the weak ego in the sense of a rigid superego. However, this cannot prevent the occurrence of states of deep inner emptiness. The consumption of violent porn videos can be seen as an addiction to combat depression.

1 I walked down the street in the darkness, on both sides small houses behind fences. Lots of barking dogs jumped against the fences. I was frightened, but then I became brave. I barked like a dog myself aggressively, and the dogs immediately fell silent.

2 I am on my way with my bicycle up a hill. It is demanding. Around me are large trees; it's like in the mountains. Arriving on top there is a little white poodle; it barks, it is on a leash. I'm driving home downhill in sharp curves. Doberman dogs are behind me. I cannot get rid of them because of the curves. They run at my side and bark at me. Then it is light and sunny; arriving on the pass it's beautiful. There is a restaurant, like in Italy, beautiful houses. On top of the pass the black dogs are coming.

3   There is stillwater, a little bridge, somebody on the other side. He falls into the water; he somehow slipped as if under a log. I pull him out, but first I hesitate. He is like dead. But that guy has a sharp knife and he cuts the other helper's throat. I flee.

4   In black and white: at a nearby train station. A girl and another person, who seems to be masochistic, and a very energetic black dog. The dog pulls the other person into the little pond, then pulls the person out of the water and up the hill. The person gives himself a blow job, then to the dog. Then I am at the foot of a tall building. I say: the dog must be put on a leash. The masochistic person says: you have to stroke the dog. I say: no, it must be put on a leash and then removed. The masochistic person is angry and goes into the tall building. The other person says: you have to follow him, he is sad. The dog smells. I put him on a leash but it is disgusting.

5   An elderly, badly smelling dog is with me and my girlfriend in Paris. It just found us. We get on the bus, the badly smelling dog could not go with us; we left it outside. We are already outside of the city limits but will return to the city on the highway. The dog would not have been able to come along behind us.

6   I was the manager of a café in the house. I was promoted like Joseph in the house of Potifar. Everybody says goodbye to a father with his little son; he's in the backyard. There is an elderly man with a Pitbull. He says: I can show you how evil the dog is. But I just had to go. I walked into a vineyard. The dog runs from its leash and goes behind me, but I jump over fences and walls. The path goes uphill through the yard and back down on the other side.

7   In a country restaurant. Two Romanians come in and start begging. I remember: the last time the two of them were masked and committed a robbery. I drive away with the motorcycle. I want to report to the police because now I know their faces.

8   A little baby is in danger. I cover it with newspaper and carry it with me through a sewerage system. Then I forget about it and leave it somewhere. But then I realize that the baby is missing and go back and find it again. I carry it with me and feed it. I think: the baby is so small, it should get mother's milk, but I can just feed him solid food.

9   I'm sitting on the couch in the garden. A man with two bot-
    tles of beer is by my side and offers one to me, maybe my
    father? I get the feeling of being unfair to the other person.
    We are having a beer together.
10 My father dies at the age of 49 years. I'm not moved at all. It
    was strange that he died so young. We don't have such a long
    life as my grandma with her 102 years of age.
11 I saw a giant toe and found it is my toe. The skin on the nail
    was grown very wide. I thought: this has to be removed. It
    could be moved back easily. There was another level of skin
    below, this one could be taken off easily, too. I was surprised
    that it did not hurt. Below the skin were very small black
    worms, everything was rotten, but you could remove it with-
    out difficulty. Below that everything was new.

From a psychodynamic point of view, the dog embodies a
threatening complex of the patient, at least in the first dreams of
the series (pattern 2). On the one hand, the experience with the
violent father is obviously reflected in this complex; the experience
of real threat through the father's unpredictable violence is con-
cretely reflected in the threat posed by the dogs. On the other
hand, the aggressiveness of the dogs also clearly reflects the
patient's own destructive violence, which, at least at the beginning
of the therapy, is not yet really mastered and controlled by the ego
and therefore repeatedly threatens and questions the ego's ability
to control itself. Interestingly, the symbol of the dog – representing
promiscuous sexuality in many cultures – also reflects the multi-
layered significance of obsessive sexuality in the patient's life, both
in his fascination with his father's obsession and in his own sexually driven behavior. The dog as the gatekeeper to the underworld
is really a striking symbol of the patient's ambivalent and unresolved relationship to his own "subterranean" impulses of libidi-
nous sexuality and violence.
    The dream series clearly shows that in the course of the ther-
apy – and presumably also due to the therapeutic process – the
meaning of the symbol slowly changes as well as the relationship
between the ego and the complex. Over time, the positive aspects
of   the   symbol,   in   particular   the   relational   function,   are

increasingly expressed. It becomes less and less threatening but needier (dreams 4 and 5), the ego is not frightened anymore but asked to relate to this needy part of its own personality in a caring way. Initially, the ego still finds this difficult and is dominated by disgust and rejection towards these parts of the personality. However, as the therapy progresses, the ego finally succeeds in behaving in a more caring and relational way towards this part, whereupon it also changes from the animal form to the human form of an infant, which can be understood psychodynamically as a development towards greater integration. The baby dream is a typical example of the dream motif of the child, which often marks turning points in therapy (Roesler, forthcoming): The baby appears as if out of nowhere; the dream ego should actually take care of it, tries, succeeds more or less, but the effort to take care of it is decisive. The dream can be clearly described as a turning point both within the entire psychotherapy and within the series of dreams. In the following dreams (pattern 5), the dreamer comes to terms with the father, with whom something like a reconciliation takes place, then the father (who is actually still alive) "dies", i.e. the issue can be psychologically buried. In the final dream, the dream ego successfully gets rid of rotten parts and emerges undamaged and renewed, an image of transformation and rebirth. This is consistent with the outcome of the therapy: The patient had meanwhile married, started a family, completed solid vocational training and acquired a good attitude in a thoroughly differentiated profession, and was well integrated socially and professionally in every respect. Although depressive moods still occurred from time to time, the patient was then increasingly able to turn to his partner with this neediness and use less violent pornography to cope with these situations.

Empirical verification of the theoretical model

As already mentioned, the typology of dream patterns was obtained inductively in a series of detailed individual case analyses. In a next step, the central hypotheses of the theoretical model were tested, namely that in cases in which the therapy is successful, an upward movement through the dream patterns can be found in the course of the dream series, and a gain in agency of the dream ego takes place (Figure 10.1). The theoretical model was tested using a sample of 86 case reports (with a total of 1290 dreams) from the archives of a psychoanalytic institute.

The typology of dream patterns (Table 10.1) was used as a coding system for the investigation of the dream series, and values were assigned to the categories. Each dream series was coded by at least two independent raters; the interrater reliability (Cohen's Kappa) was k =.70 -.82. The hypotheses of the theoretical model were tested using various statistical methods and were found to be statistically confirmed (for a detailed description, see Roesler et al., 2024).

For all cases individually, a regression line was calculated using the non-parametric Spearman rank correlation (independent (metric) variable sequence of dreams over time (1-X) and dependent (ordinal) variable dream pattern) as well as the slope of the regression line over the entire dream series (see below, Figure 10.2, for an example). For 66% of the successful therapies, the hypothesis was confirmed that there is an upward movement parallel to the course of therapy with different effect sizes (r =.45 -.84, p <.05). In general, the lower dream patterns (1, 2 and 3) are more frequent in the first half of therapy and decrease towards the end of therapy, while higher-order dream patterns (4, 5 and 6) increasingly dominate in the second half. Typically, a case begins with dreams of type 2, and the last dream in the series is usually a dream type 5 or 6. Failed cases, on the other hand, typically show a decreasing regression line, while unsuccessful cases show no correlation at all.

Amalia X

The methodology of SDA was applied also to the case Amalia X mentioned above. Earlier studies of the case (Kächele et al., 1999) found characteristic transformations over the course of the dream series: The later the session in treatment occurred, the more "[...] of the text of the dreams was attended to and worked over cognitively" (p. 8). Positive self-esteem increased significantly during the course of treatment, although the trend did not set in right at the start of treatment but only after wide fluctuations over the first

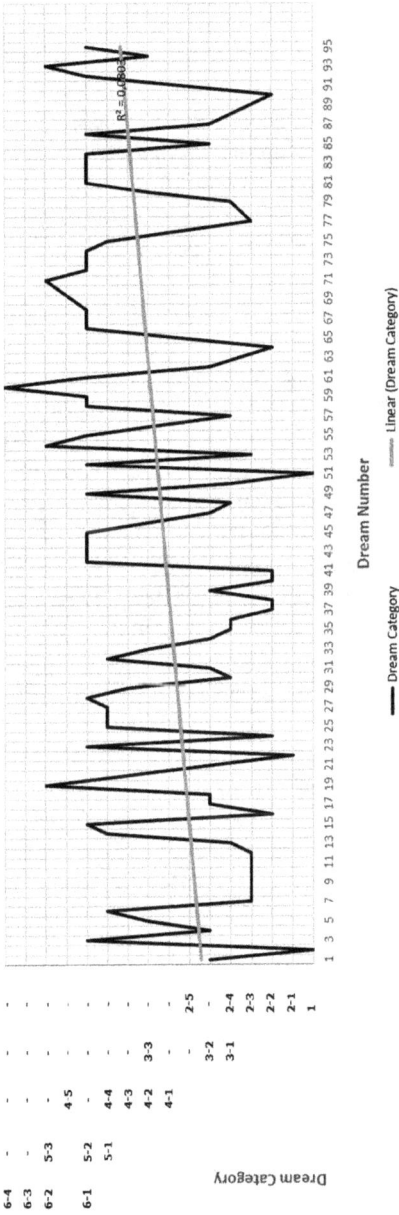

Figure 10.2 Amalia X, distribution of dream patterns and regression line

100 sessions; also, negative self-esteem showed a significant and continuous decrease from the beginning of treatment. They also identified a steady trend from negative dream emotions at the beginning to positive emotions towards the end of the analysis, as well as a steady systematic change in the problem-solving activity of the dream ego escalating as the analysis proceeds. Gennaro et al. (2020) confirmed that over the course of the dream series the patient got progressively more access to affective-laden unconscious dimensions.

In the statistical analysis of the 95 dreams, each dream was coded independently by two raters (Cohen's Kappa Coefficient, $k = 0.814$, $p < .001$). As it is considered to be a very successful therapy, a significant upwards movement from lower to higher patterns was expected as well as a gain in initiative of the dream ego. This was statistically confirmed: Nonparametric Spearman Rank Correlation is significant, $r = .29$, $p = .003$ (see Figure 10.2). There is an accumulation of dreams pattern 2 in the first phase of therapy, whereas the second half of therapy is dominated by pattern 5. One of the last dreams is a character-istic autonomy dream (pattern 6), in which the dreamer walks on her hairs (note the specific disorder of hirsutismus) into the practice of her analyst, says goodbye and leaves on her own, contently autonomous.

Our findings regarding the patterns that dominated the first half of therapy parallel findings by Albani et al. (2003) using the Core Conflictual Relationship Theme method (CCRT): They found significant changes in the narratives at the end of therapy express-ing more autonomy, and a reduction of experiences of being dependent and weak, unable to set limits and frustrated.

The case C.L.

The well-known German psychoanalyst Alexander Mitscherlich (1983) published the well-documented case C.L. containing 103 dreams which were discussed over the course of therapy together with a detailed case description. The case is considered highly suc-cessful and was published to be used in research. The 28-year-old female patient was treated because of sleep disturbances, depression, anxieties, psychosomatic symptoms (e.g. unexplained fever attacks) and diverse sexual problems (e.g. vaginismus), which are apparently connected to repeated experiences of sexual assault during adolescence.

The above-mentioned hypotheses were tested for this case using the Nonparametric Spearman Rank Correlation. Interrater reliability for the coding of the dreams was found to be good (k = 0.854, p <.001). The results supported the hypothesis that there is a positive correlation between the sequence of dreams and level of dream pattern (r =.30; p < 0.01). Parallel to the progress of therapy, there is a movement from lower to higher dream patterns, with the second half of therapy being dominated by patterns 4 and 5. Over the course of therapy, the dream ego increasingly succeeds in coping with tasks, solving problems and creating satisfying social interactions; there is a continuous increase in dream ego agency (r =.43; p < 0.001).

Based on the dreams alone, a psychological profile of the dreamer was created which correctly predicted the symptoms and psychological problems described in the case report. The images and topics appearing repeatedly in the dreams provided an accurate picture of the psychological conflicts of the patient as well as of therapeutic change over the course of therapy. For example, a major topic in the dream series is encounters with men, which in the first half of the dream series are generally unpleasant and, in many cases, even threatening. This motif changes over the course of therapy; encounters with men become more satisfying, and by the end of the dream series men even become rescuers of the dream ego in threatening situations (change in the motif from pattern 2 to pattern 5 dreams). This runs parallel to the changes in the real-life relationships of the patient, as reported by Mitscherlich (1983). In contrast to the case of Amalia X, here the beginning of the series of dreams contains a number of pattern 1 dreams, which would speak for a low level of ego strength. This is confirmed by the case report arguing for a more severe disorder of self-esteem in the patient.

Chapter 11

Conclusion

What do these empirical findings mean for psychoanalytic dream theories?

First of all, it must be noted that even if the results of dream research presented above can be interesting and helpful for psychoanalytic theory-building in many respects, there are fundamental differences in perspective. For example, empirical dream research is far removed from the model assumed by psychoanalysis, namely that dreams primarily serve to process unconscious content in the sense of psychodynamics. When dream research talks about insight, it tends to mean cognitive problem solving and therefore something completely different from psychoanalysis. On the other hand, many psychoanalytic dream theorists have a certain resistance to acknowledging the findings of dream research, whether clinical or non-clinical, and consequently revise or even abandon their own favored theories. Psychoanalytic authors also point to this problem:

> The pitfalls of clinical psychoanalytic research are well known. They range from the random selection and summarization of clinical material in order to substantiate certain theoretical views, to hermetically sealed lines of argumentation, narcissistic considerations instead of self-critical, open reflections on clinical observations, to the presentation of psychoanalytic 'star cases' instead of normal or even failed treatments. Furthermore, there is [...] the danger of an (unconscious) construction of desired psychoanalytic insights that correspond to prevailing theoretical concepts and thus confirm them again and again.
>
> (Fischmann, Leuzinger-Bohleber & Kächele, 2012, p. 838; transl. C.R.)

DOI: 10.4324/9781003492078-12

In my opinion, some of the questions raised at the beginning can nowadays be answered to a large extent based on the results of dream research. Some of the assumptions of psychoanalysis are confirmed – sometimes quite impressively – but classical psychoanalytical positions must also at least be relativized, if not abandoned.

On the one hand, the psychoanalytical dream theory also makes nomothetic claims; for example, regarding the function of dreaming for night-time sleep. On the other hand, an overview of the results of dream research reveals a coherent theory of explanation in some areas. In the following, the questions that are important for the debate on dream theories and their use in psychotherapy will be discussed against the background of the research results. This will then lead to an attempt to develop a coherent psychological theory of the function of dreams for the regulation of the psyche. The central finding, however, is that psychoanalysis has been fundamentally correct in its view that dreams have meaning, are closely related to the dreamer's waking life and his emotional concerns and problems, and have a psychological function for the whole organism. This thesis was first formulated by Freud in his *Interpretation of Dreams*, which gives him the credit for initiating a modern theory of the phenomenon of dreams and their use in psychotherapy.

The German psychoanalysts Werner and Langenmayr (2005) show in their major review of the significance of empirical findings for Freud's dream theory that Freud's fundamental assumption that dreams have a psychological meaning and are closely linked to the dreamer's life is comprehensively empirically supported. However, they emphasize that the significance of the manifest dream is clearly enhanced by the empirical literature and that the importance of the dreamer's associations in clarifying the meaning must be relativized: "Aspects essential to the dreamer's person can also be inferred from the manifest dream. It is not plausible to assume a fundamental difference between dream and waking state with regard to the function and interpretability of the contents" (p. 170; transl. C.R.). They also cite a number of findings that question Freud's assumption about the protective function of dreams for sleep. They also emphasize that more recent research findings show a great similarity between dream sleep and the function of waking consciousness, which is difficult to reconcile with Freud's view.

Overall, the psychoanalytic assumptions, which were revolutionary in Freud's time, that dreams are closely related to waking life and in particular to the dreamer's problems, and that they provide information that can be used psychotherapeutically, are thus impressively confirmed empirically. Jung's thesis that during sleep the unconscious has a greater amount of information and connecting capacity than the limited conscious mind and is therefore more capable of suggesting solutions or at least providing clues to the conscious mind that take the overall psyche and its situation into account is also surprisingly clearly demonstrated.

Dreams have psychological meaning

An initial key insight gained from the comparison of dream research and psychoanalysis is that the following has been impressively proven: Dreams have fundamental meaning and are not meaningless idle brain activity. Numerous studies prove the close connection not only between dreams and the dreamer's waking life but also with emotionally significant and stressful topics and inner conflicts of the dreamer. This confirms the basic assumptions of all psychoanalytical schools, but especially the pioneering work of Freud.

Dreaming (REM sleep) is biologically indispensable for the organism and must therefore also have a function for the psyche and mental functioning. There is evidence that the deliberate prevention of dream sleep leads to psychological problems in those affected. Empirically, there is also a clear connection between waking life experiences and the content of dreams. It can also be shown that the dream content primarily addresses the dreamer's problems, especially those with a high emotional relevance for the dreamer. In this respect, the basic psychoanalytical approach of attributing a psychological meaning to dreams and using them for therapeutic purposes is justified.

Dreaming serves psychological self-regulation

Dreams have a function through which emotions are regulated in a positive direction. They also help us to cope with stressful events in waking life. In addition, they apparently serve to consolidate memory and thus the functioning of consciousness. This would tend to support Jung's view, or more recent (e.g. self-psychological) theories on dreams, according to which they serve the self-regulation of the psyche – in contrast to Freud's model.

What does the dream take up? Experiences of the day, especially those with emotional significance or even stressful affects, are reactivated from short-term memory during dreaming and compared with earlier experiences from long-term memory; in particular, how similar experiences and conflicts were resolved or overcome in earlier situations. This would initially confirm Freud's basic assumption that dreams link current events (day residue) with previous experiences, especially those that are emotionally stressful. However, Freud may have underestimated the solution orientation and coping power of dreams at this point. This is emphasized more by Jung, and current psychoanalytical dream theories move in this direction.

Dreams promote insights and creative problem solving: Dreams have been shown to promote creativity and provide impetus for insights and problem solving in waking life – and not just in rare exceptional cases. Dreams demonstrably deal with the person's problems from waking life and attempt to develop solutions to these problems by drawing on experiences stored in memory. Empirical research thus supports the views of Jung and more recent psychoanalytic authors, e.g. Hartmann, that insights and possible solutions to psychological problems are brought to consciousness in dreams.

Dreams make use of the more comprehensive knowledge of the unconscious: Dreams can create more far-reaching associative links than thinking in the waking state, partly because more areas of the brain are involved in "dream thinking" than in waking life. This is very close to Jung's theory that the unconscious, which produces dreams, has a more comprehensive knowledge or perspective than the conscious mind. Thinking further, this would actually confirm the usefulness of the psychoanalytical method of collecting associations or Jung's method of amplification in dream interpretation, as they create a far-reaching network of associations rather than a targeted determination of meaning. However, whether these far-reaching associations in dreams are directly involved in insights or problem solving cannot be clearly deduced from the empirical research results.

Apparently, in contrast to waking consciousness, the brain is able to activate and link larger areas and more functions simultaneously during sleep. This makes it easier to find new solutions in dreams than in focused waking consciousness. This is also confirmed by a review by the empirical dream researcher Barrett (2001): In dreams, the brain can switch to a processing mode in which it no longer has to constantly process new input as it does in the waking state. This frees up more capacity to deal with unresolved problems and work on them creatively.

Empirical research thus supports some central statements of psychoanalysis and Jung in particular. This confirms Jung's thesis that during sleep the unconscious has a greater amount of information and linking capacity than the limited conscious mind and is therefore more capable of suggesting solutions or at least providing clues to the conscious mind that take the overall psyche and its situation into account.

However, it also raises questions: For example, it could be argued on the basis of the research results that it is not absolutely necessary for the dreamer to remember the dreams in order to achieve the psychological benefits that dreaming apparently provides – at least this applies to the emotion-regulating, memory-consolidating and learning-promoting effects of dreaming. However, this in turn would contradict a central argument in psychoanalytic dream theory, namely that dreams have a healing effect primarily through the transmission of information from the unconscious to the conscious mind, that making the unconscious conscious is decisive.

Self-representation rather than concealment

In accordance with the continuity hypothesis of waking and dreaming states of today's experimental dream research (Schredl, 2006), the question already raised between Jung and Freud as to whether the dream contains a coded meaning (Freud) or expresses it symbolically in the best possible way (Jung) can be decided quite clearly in Jung's favor. There is nothing to suggest that a coding or distorting activity takes place in dream sleep. Physical stimuli that occur during sleep are incorporated into the dream but are not distorted; they are expressed in a pictorial-like manner. In a series of empirical studies, the two Freudian psychoanalysts Glucksman and Kramer (2015) have explicitly investigated the question of whether the manifest content of dreams is sufficient to understand the psychodynamics of the dreamer and to describe changes in the patient's symptomatology in the context of psychotherapy. First, they note that there is a strong parallel between the known functions of dreams, particularly problem and conflict resolution, affect regulation, learning and coping, and self-awareness, and the crucial variables responsible for change in psychotherapy. It must therefore be assumed that there is a connection between the two dimensions. The results of their systematic studies show that the manifest content of dreams changes in parallel with clinical change in the course of psychotherapeutic treatment, especially when the structure of the dream narrative is examined. Similarly, the affects represented in the dream behave in parallel with the change in affects during the course of treatment. The first dream (initial dream) of a treatment can also be used to make a valid prediction not only about the decisive themes in the course of the therapy but also about the outcome and the improvement achieved. Finally, the dreams alone can be used to create a correct formulation of the patient's psychodynamics, which corresponds to the assessment of the treating therapist and with the topics that are worked on during the course of therapy. In conclusion, they state that the significance of the manifest dream content must be fundamentally reconsidered within psychoanalysis.

Fisher and Greenberg (1977, 1996), although Freudians and more concerned with finding evidence for Freud's theses in empirical studies, also state in view of the overwhelming amount of data that the meaning of the dream lies more in the manifest content and is not encoded or distorted.

Numerous more recent psychoanalytic theories also speak directly of the self-representational function of dreams, e.g. Kohut (1977), Stolorow (1978), Fosshage (1987), Fiss (1995), the control-mastery theory and, very early on, Fairbairn (1952). Most of these authors also attribute self-regulatory abilities to dreams, in particular Hartmann (1995, 1998) in his work on nightmares. However, this does not only apply to nightmares. There is at least one empirically ascertainable type of dream, so-called "low-structured dreams", which regularly indicate severe regression states or personality disorders in the dreamer (Ermann, 2005) and present their meaning completely undisguised. In accordance with experimental dream research and its view of the continuity between waking and dreaming, the day residue is given the actual meaning in today's psychoanalytical dream interpretation as opposed to the reductionist search for the hidden infantile wish behind the dream. Starting from the day residue, associations with the dreamer are used to work out the connections to the past, the present and the current therapeutic situation. Instead of the fulfillment of infantile instinctual desires, dreams today are seen more as self-expression and an attempt to solve problems (Kohut, 1977; Moser, 1999). In self-psychology in the tradition of Kohut (1977), it is assumed, in agreement with the view in Jung, that the psyche has a capacity for self-regulation. The function of the dream is then seen as stabilizing or restoring the psychic organization in the event of threats to the integrity of the self by depicting the inner-psychic situation in the dream, concretizing it pictorially, so to speak.

Fosshage (1987, 1997) has formulated a modern psychoanalytical theory of dreams on the basis of the findings of empirical dream research and neuroscience referred to here. According to this theory, the most important functions of dreaming are the development, maintenance and reintegration of the psychic organization. Dreams are able to effectively regulate emotions, develop solutions to current conflict situations and rebalance the psychological structure. Through its imaginations, the dream can provide a picture of psychological development processes that are still inaccessible to the conscious mind. Fosshage openly acknowledges the great analogies to Jung's theory: His view of the self-regulating and problem-solving function of dreams corresponds to Jung's concept of the compensatory function; his idea of the imaging of still unconscious developmental processes in dreams corresponds to Jung's prospective function.

"Guardian of sleep" or creative problem solver?

Some psychoanalytic researchers argue on the basis of their own empirical studies that Freud's assumption of the protective function of dreams for sleep can be empirically proven (Solms, 2013a; Ermann, 1995). However, an overview of the results of dream research on this question shows that this is a rather isolated position. The vast majority of dream researchers, including psychoanalytic authors (e.g. Werner & Langenmayr, 2005), interpret the empirical findings as refuting Freud's view.

The dream is clearly not the guardian of sleep, as Freud assumed; it is rather the other way around – that we need REM sleep. This is because when REM sleep is deprived, the organism makes up for it to a greater extent on subsequent nights. In this respect, sleep is the guardian of dreams (Schredl, 2006). Accordingly, the psychoanalyst Berner also summarizes the results in his overview of empirical dream research: "The protection of sleep does not appear to be a function of the almost constantly occurring dreams" (Berner, 2018, p. 113).

In the presentation of empirical dream research, it has become clear that dreaming generally has a regulatory function for the organism. Both Freud's and Jung's dream theories could be described as regulation theories – albeit with a different focus. Freud's dream theory could be described as a theory of local regulation: During sleep, unconscious affects, wishes etc. push out of the unconscious and threaten the psychic equilibrium, and therefore must be transformed through dream work from a threatening to a harmless state, i.e. from latent to manifest content. Regulation therefore takes place locally, so to speak, i.e. at the moment of sleep and ultimately serves to regulate sleep at night.

In Jung's dream theory, on the other hand, the focus is on compensation in the service of the individuation process, which is why it could be described as a theory of global regulation: In dreams, the unconscious confronts the conscious mind with one-sidedness, missing, split-off or underdeveloped aspects of the personality, with the aim of achieving wholeness of the person. In this respect, dreams of the same night and over longer periods of time repeatedly revolve around the same themes. The goal is a longer-term development or completion of the overall personality, and in this respect the regulation in Jung's theory is aimed at a global goal.

Both assumptions are supported by empirical dream research and the theories developed from it. On the one hand, it can be shown that during sleep, difficult affects are actually processed and mitigated in the dream itself, which supports Freud's view in the broadest sense. However, many research results can also be understood as supporting Jung's thesis that dreaming also has an integrating function for the personality as a whole beyond the local regulation of affects during the night and thus promotes its global development.

However, the constructive contribution of dreaming also plays a role in Freud's theory insofar as the dream by taking up day-time events that have in turn activated unconscious wishes or conflicts addresses these and thus makes them fundamentally accessible to consciousness. On the other hand, Freud also assumes that emotionally activating events in dreams are placed in a wider associative context and that the dream processes unconscious content and thus promotes further development, at least by creating a potential for awareness. Some of the studies and theories from dream research listed above could be seen as a confirmation of Freud's assumption that primary process thinking is at work in dreams. At the very least, it can be confirmed that although dreaming is a form of thinking, it is qualitatively different from thinking in the waking state, for example due to the neurotransmitters present.

Overall, however, it can be shown quite clearly from the description of dream research that dreams obviously do indeed contain a strong problem-solving activity that is able to effectively deal with psychological tensions and conflicts of the person's waking life and thus not only achieve a psychological regulatory performance but even advance the development of the personality in the direction of stronger integration and a balancing of inner psychic forces. This clearly speaks more in favor of Jung's position and that of contemporary psychoanalytic dream theories, e.g. from self-psychology, while Freud had obviously underestimated this problem-solving power of dreaming.

Wish fulfillment theory

With reference to the dreams of American soldiers in Japanese captivity, in which they fantasized themselves into a powerful position and images of liberation and satisfaction prevailed, Weiss (1993) argues that here the dreamers had obtained relief in their hopeless situation through a fantasized wish fulfillment, which is seen as evidence for Freud's wish fulfillment theory. Another proponent is the neuropsychoanalyst Solms (2013a, 2013b), who believes he can prove the wish-fulfilling function of dreams based on his studies on brain-damaged patients.

According to Fischmann and Leuschner (2008), the wish fulfillment theory cannot be proven experimentally. Although they report a small amount of research evidence for the wish fulfillment theory, many more results clearly contradict it, which Freud himself had to admit in relation to post-traumatic dreams. From the very beginning, there were also numerous critics of wish fulfillment theory within psychoanalysis: If one wanted to, dreams could always be interpreted in such a way that wish fulfillment would ultimately result – this was an immunization strategy of psychoanalysis (overview in Boothe & Stojkovic, 2013). However, this also applies to Jung's compensation thesis. Although the presentation of empirical dream research shows that dreams can certainly be attributed regulative functions, it is still unclear what exactly is being regulated: Does it only serve relaxation, problem solving, the consolidation of memories, etc.? As a result of the findings of empirical dream research, psychoanalysis now ascribes a number of other dream functions to dreams in addition to wish fulfillment, including memory consolidation, problem solving, stress reduction, creativity, conflict resolution and affect regulation (Kächele, 2012).

Does the dream compensate?

The continuity thesis of waking and dream life as the conclusion of experimental dream research tends to speak against the compensation thesis. Even in the examples from dream research presented above, including the methodology of structural dream analysis, no evidence of compensation by the dream could be found. Rather, the dream actually depicts – often in a drastic way – the partly unconscious psychological problems of the dreamer. In his treatise on Jung's dream theory in the light of research, Vedfelt (1997) comes to the interesting conclusion

> that the contrast/continuation debate [i.e. compensation versus continuity, author's note] is too simplistic when measured against the actual complexity of the dream phenomenon [, and furthermore] the different creativity of professional dream interpreters – as opposed to rigid frames of reference – plays a role in what is interpreted as contrasting with waking consciousness and waking life.
>
> (p. 278)

In my view, the following epistemological obstacle generally applies to both theses, wish fulfillment and compensation respectively: Psychoanalytic dream interpretation represents a hermeneutic and thus is always placed in the world of subjective, at best interpersonal, structures of meaning and is thus categorically different from the world of objective facts. For this reason, the fundamental question is whether the two theses are even accessible for examination in the nomothetic research paradigm. The very question of what the dreamer's current problem situation is, to which a dream element could then stand in a compensatory relationship, is to a large extent a result of the interpretation of subjective contexts of meaning. For example, the same symptomatology may represent a painful problem for one person but not at all for another. The same applies to the wish fulfillment thesis: The question of what the latent, unconscious (instinctual) wish is that is represented in a veiled form in the dream and at the same time satisfied is the result of an interpretation within the framework of the analytic relationship – in other words, an intersubjective meaning. Fischer (1978) was able to show in a comparison of patient dreams of Freudian and Jungian analysts that the theoretical position of the analyst had an indirect effect on the content of the patient's dreams: If the therapist is a Freudian, typical Freudian symbolism is more likely to be found, i.e. in the broadest sense interpretable as sexual symbolism; if the therapist is a Jungian, typical archetypal symbolism is found. This would suggest that even dream generation is an interpersonal event (Kron & Avny, 2003).

Dream interpretation as hermeneutics

At this point, it is crucial to distinguish between clinical practice, which ultimately aims to change the subjective experience of the patient, and scientific research, which aims to formulate general laws and correlations. For clinical practice, it makes perfect sense to use a thesis such as wish fulfillment or compensation as an interpretative strategy, in order to use the dream in a therapeutic sense and thus open up new perspectives on oneself for the patient. Accordingly, psychoanalysis has always emphasized that the criterion of the "correctness" of the interpretation is ultimately always the patient's reaction – which does not necessarily mean conscious consent but the response of a subject that creates meaning. It follows from this that any kind of verification of the compensation thesis, as well as the wish fulfillment thesis, always presupposes interpretative processes. On the other hand, it also follows that working with dreams in the context of psychotherapy, especially psychoanalytical dream interpretation, must always be seen as a hermeneutic that does not reconstruct objective facts, but rather subjective meanings – and this is legitimate in the context of psychotherapy. Freud's famous junction of healing and research must, however, be fundamentally questioned against this background.

Towards a research-informed theory of dreams

Essential Freudian assumptions must be regarded as refuted. The dream researcher Fiss (1995), himself a Freudian, states in his review of the significance of empirical findings for Freud's dream theory that the following Freudian assumptions could not be confirmed experimentally: The wish fulfillment theory, the assumptions about the difference and connection between latent and manifest dream content, the thesis of the dream as the guardian of sleep and the role of repression in dream work. The

German psychoanalysts Werner and Langenmayr (2005) come to practically the same conclusion in their major review of psychoanalysis and empiricism. In my opinion, the reported empirical research results and the convergence of the Freudian view of dreams with Jung's make it clear that Jung's dream theory was, on the one hand, quite forward-looking, as it anticipates many later findings. On the other hand, it becomes clear, especially in comparison with Freud's dream theory, that Jung took a fairly level-headed and detached stance on the subject of dreams, formulated a theory that was close to "common sense" and made little recourse to complicated explanatory mechanisms (such as dream censorship). At least this is true if one takes his first dream theory, according to which the dream represents a self-image of the situation of the psyche, as a basis. With his compensation theory, which is very much based on his conviction that the psyche is organized in structures of opposites, his dream theory then narrowed further.

From today's perspective, it can best be summarized that the various dream theories that have been discussed so far shed light on important aspects of the meaning and function of dreams. At the same time, the function of dreams cannot be reduced to a single one of these aspects. The dream certainly plays an important role in integrative processes in the psyche. In addition, however, it also has a generative function for psychological growth and apparently even for creativity and problem solving. The importance of interpreting dreams must also be relativized in view of the regulatory performance that has become clear, which nocturnal dreaming performs completely unconsciously, in the background, so to speak.

Ermann's (2005) well-founded treatise on the current state of knowledge regarding the function of dreams, which is based on the results of empirical and neuroscientific dream research presented here, derives the following view for contemporary psychoanalytic dream work:

> When dreaming, information from completely different areas of perception and memory are connected. Unprocessed daytime impressions from waking life are perceived during sleep, e.g. an insult, a tempting situation, a task that was not

completed. These perceptions activate the centers responsible for the formation of dreams, which now begin to make contact with various memory stores and retrieve information from there. This activates memory contents that are similar to the day residue. This includes experiences and emotional states but also conflicts and problems, as well as coping strategies and solutions. [...] As a result of the dream mechanism, something new emerges that contains a better solution than the unprocessed initial information. [...] The function of the dream mechanism is primarily information processing as problem solving through re-evaluation. It is a guide to creative solutions and the practicing of coping.

(p. 68, transl. C.R.)

A compromise formula: Expansion of consciousness instead of compensation

On the basis of the reported research results and the consensus views among dream researchers, I would like to propose a reformulation of the compensation thesis in this section. The research results can be summarized with Werner and Langenmayr (2005, p. 169f.) as follows:

The dream serves to work through emotional experiences, to classify them in previous experiential contexts and to consolidate memory. [...] In this context, it can also take on the function of the hallucinatory satisfaction of wishes. The classification in previous experiential contexts draws on current, recent and much earlier experiences up to childhood. The processing of what was experienced before the dream seems to go from the current to the earlier references. The material used in the dream is unconscious to varying degrees.

In addition to the findings that the mental processes in dreams can apparently draw on more extensive connections and networks between brain areas than in the waking state, one could formulate this in accordance with Jung's statements: Dreams use more comprehensive mental functions, memories and knowledge than the waking state and can thus expand or supplement the possibly limited view of consciousness with additional information and is actually creative and oriented towards problem solving. However, this addition is not necessarily in opposition to consciousness.

In this respect, Jung's formulations of the self-imaging and compensatory functions of dreams can be combined to form a thesis according to which consciousness is expanded with new information with the help of dreams. What is not confirmed is the thesis that the more one-sided the consciousness is with regard to its problems the more critical or corrective this new information is in the dream.

The Jungian perspective on dreams could also represent a synthesis for the debate on continuity versus discontinuity of dreams and waking life in empirical dream research. In their discussion of the continuity hypothesis, Hobson and Schredl (2011) point out that dreams do indeed contain elements of waking life on a thematic level, but that this does not yet explain the occurrence of elements in dreams that the dreamer has never experienced in waking life (e.g. fantastic animals). "This raises the intriguing question: If dreaming is not entirely derived from waking experience, then just what is the source of the anomalous content and what is its function?" (Hobson & Schredl, 2011, p. 3). In his commentary on this discussion, Hoss (2011), with reference to Jung, points out that this content does not represent distortions or misrepresentations of waking life, but rather the unconscious aspect of waking experience, which is, however, represented in dreams in the form of an image.

Outlook

Many questions remain unanswered: Why do we only remember certain dreams when research clearly shows that we dream for several hours every night? Do dreams even need to be interpreted in order for them to be therapeutically effective? The research by Hartmann (1995) and Greenberg and Pearlman (1978) described above could serve as evidence that the dream itself performs a quasi-therapeutic processing of emotionally significant content, which is then also reflected in an improvement in the dreamer's symptoms.

An entirely new field of research has opened up through the study of so-called lucid dreaming, in which the dreamer knows that he or she is dreaming and can actively intervene in the dream events. This phenomenon does not appear to be rare, and it can apparently be learned. The very existence of this phenomenon naturally raises clear questions about practically all the psychoanalytical theories mentioned.

Some authors also use the phenomenon of dreams and empirical research to examine or discuss fundamental questions about the nature of the human mind and how it works. This is done within the framework of consciousness studies and the philosophy of mind (e.g. Windt, 2015, 2018). Based on the continuity hypothesis of waking and dreaming presented above, the question discussed is, for example, to what extent the ego of the dream differs from the ego of the waking state and what this says about the construction of a subjective self in general. Even if the question of how a human brain can generate and integrate a self is still unanswered, Windt (2018) postulates that sleep dreams are just as much conscious phenomenal states with a subjective quality of experience as they are felt in our waking experience. Even during dreaming there is always a subjective feeling of immediate spatial and temporal presence – the experience of a dream ego as the center of the dream world. This subjective experience structure from the internal first-person perspective is practically always a component of all types of dreams (Strauch & Meier, 2004). During dreaming, however, we do not realize that this dream world, which appears "real" to us, is merely a mental simulation. If the construction of a subjective ego does not fundamentally differ between waking and dreaming, this naturally raises the question of the extent to which our waking experience is not also largely such a mental simulation (Hau, 2018). This hypothesis appears to be underpinned by findings on the adaptive function of the Default Mode Network (Domhoff & Fox, 2015). The activities of this network start as soon as no goal-oriented mental activity is pursued – i.e. whenever we switch to an introspective processing mode such as mind-wandering and day-dreaming. It is now suspected that the default mode network could also be involved in the generation of dream processes (Hau, 2018). This in turn calls into question the rigid demarcation of the different sleep phases and thus also the separation of different mental states of consciousness. In other words: The distinction we make that daytime waking consciousness seems more real to us than consciousness in dreams can be questioned, as both are based on the same mental simulation processes (Domhoff & Schneider, 2018). Instead, it is about different forms of experience with specific characteristics and corresponding neuronal correlates (Windt, 2015, 2018). The feeling of presence created in this way, a kind of self-understanding, is intended to free us per se from the need to constantly turn our attention to conscious perception, even if our focus of attention is not required. Instead, we engage in a continuous stream of mental simulations and are immersed in such daydreams for an estimated 30–50% of our waking hours (Windt, 2015). This process seems to be only slightly affected by our perceptual and bodily experiences, which are constantly taking place at the same time. From this perspective, mind-wandering would not be a deficient state but on the contrary a normal, essential and health-promoting mental activity – just like dreaming (Windt, 2015). It is therefore possible that the difference between the two activities is smaller than we think (Windt, 2018).

Thus, despite all the theorizing and empirical research, the dream remains a mystery – both enigmatic and fascinating.

References

Adler, A. (2010). *Persönlichkeitstheorie, Psychopathologie, Psychotherapie (1913–1937)*. Göttingen: Vandenhoeck & Ruprecht.

Albani, C., Pokorny, D., Blaser, G., König, S., Thomä, H. & Kächele, H. (2003). Study of a psychoanalytic process using the Core Conflictual Relationship Theme (CCRT) method according to the Ulm Process Model. *European Psychotherapy*, 4, 11–32.

Alexander, F. G. (1925). Über Traumpaare und Traumreihen. *Internationale Zeitschrift für Psychoanalyse*, 11, 80–85.

Angeloch, D. (2020). Den Traum denken: Traum und Traumdenken bei Sigmund Freud, Hanna Segal und Wilfred Bion. In M. Guthmüller & H. W. Schmidt-Hannisa (eds.), *Das Nächtliche Selbst* (pp. 77–108). Göttingen: Wallstein Verlag.

Aserinsky, E. & Kleitman, N. (1953). Regularly occurring periods of eye motility and concomitant phenomena during sleep. *Science*, 118, 273–274.

Barrett, D. (1996). Dreams in Multiple Personality. In D. Barrett (ed.), *Trauma and Dreams*. Cambridge: Harvard University Press.

Barrett, D. (2001). *The Committee of Sleep: How Artists, Scientists, and Athletes use Dreams for Creative Problem Solving*. New York: Crown.

Barrett, D. (2015). Dreams: Thinking in a Different Biochemical State. In M. Kramer & M. Glucksman (eds.), *Dream Research: Contributions to Clinical Practice* (pp. 80–94). London: Routledge.

Barrett, D. & McNamara, P. (2007). *The New Science of Dreaming: Vol. 2. Content, Recall, Personality Correlates*. Westport: Praeger.

Bash, K. W. (1988/1950). Zur experimentellen Grundlegung der Jungschen Traumanalyse. In K. W. Bash (eds.), *Die analytische Psychologie im Umfeld der Wissenschaften* (pp. 145–154). Bern: Huber.

Berner, W. (2018). Empirische Traumforschung. In W. Berner, G. Amelung, A. Boll-Klatt & U. Lamperter (eds.), *Von Irma zu Amalie: Der*

Traum und seine psychoanalytische Bedeutung im Wandel der Zeit (pp. 111–120). Giessen: Psychosozial.

Berner, W., Amelung, G., Boll-Klatt, A. & Lamperter, U. (2018). *Von Irma zu Amalie: Der Traum und seine psychoanalytische Bedeutung im Wandel der Zeit.* Giessen: Psychosozial.

Binswanger, R. & Wittmann, L. (2019). Reconsidering Freud's dream theory. *International Journal of Dream Research,* 12(1), 103–111.

Bion, W. R. (1962). A Theory of Thinking. In E. Bott-Spillius (eds.), *Melanie Klein Today* (pp. 178–186). London: Routledge.

Bion, W. R. (1967). *Cogitations.* London: Karnac.

Blanck, G. & Blanck, R. (1974). *Ego Psychology: Theory and Practice.* New York: Columbia University Press.

Bódizs, R., Simor, P., Csóka, S., Bérdi, M. & Kopp, M. (2008). Dreaming and health promotion: A theoretical proposal and some epidemiological establishments. *European Journal of Mental Health,* 3(1), 35–62.

Bohleber, W. (2012). Neue Befunde zum Traum und seine Bedeutung. *Psyche,* 66, 769–775.

Bollas, C. (1987). *Der Schatten des Objekts: Das ungedachte Bekannte: zur Psychoanalyse der frühen Entwicklung.* Stuttgart: Klett Cotta.

Boothe, B. (2002). *Kodiermanual zur Erzählanalyse JAKOB: Berichte aus der Klinischen Psychologie.* Zurich: Universität Zürich, Psychologisches Institut.

Boothe, B. (2006). Körpererleben in der Traummitteilung und Körpererfahrung im Traum. *PiD-Psychotherapie im Dialog,* 7(2), 185–190.

Boothe, B. (2018). Amalie – Traumdeutung in der heutigen Praxis. In W. Berner, G. Amelung, A. Boll-Klatt & U. Lamparter (eds.), *Von Irma zu Amalie, der Traum und seine psychoanalytische Bedeutung im Wandel der Zeit* (pp. 53–83). Giessen: Psychosozial-Verlag.

Boothe, B. & Stojkovic, D. (2013). Schlafhüter und Muntermacher – Traum, Wunsch und die Kunst des Wartens. In B. Boothe (eds.), *Wenn doch nur – ach hätte ich bloß: Die Anatomie des Wunsches* (pp. 34–70). Zurich: Rüffer & Rub.

Bradlow, P. A. & Bender, E. P. (1997). Frist dreams in psychoanalysis. *A Case Study Journal of Clinical Psychoanalysis,* 12, 387–396.

Bulkeley, K. (2007). Sacred Sleep: Scientific Contributions to the Study of Religiously Significant Dreaming. In D. Barrett & P. McNamara (eds.), *The New Science of Dreaming: Cultural and Theoretical Perspectives* (pp. 71–94). Westport: Praeger.

Bulkeley, K. (2008). *Dreaming in the World's Religions.* New York: New York University Press.

Carr, M., Heymann, R., Lisson, A., Werne, N. M. & Schredl, M. (2022). Nightmare frequency and nightmare distress: Relationship to the big five personality factors and sensory-processing sensitivity. *Dreaming*, 32 (3), 257–268.

Cartwright, R. D. (1977). *Night Life*. Englewood Cliffs: Prentice-Hall.

Cartwright, R. D. (1991). Dreams that work: The relation of dream incorporation to adaptation to stressful events. *Journal of Dreaming*, 1, 3–9.

Cartwright, R. D. (1996). Dreams and the Adaptation to Divorce. In D. Barrett (eds.), *Trauma and Dreams* (pp. 179–185). Cambridge: Harvard University Press.

Cartwright, R. (2005). Dreaming as a Mood Regulation System. In M. Kryger, T. Roth & W. Dement (eds.), *Principles and Practice of Sleep Medicine* (pp. 565–572). Philadelphia: Elsevier Saunders.

Cartwright, R. D., Luten, A., Young, M., Mercer, P. & Bears, M. (1998). Role of REM-sleep and dream affect in overnight mood regulation: A study of normal volunteers. *Psychiatry Research*, 81, 1–8.

Cogar, M. C., & Hill, C. E. (1992). Examining the effects of brief dream interpretation. *Dreaming*, 2, 239–248.

Crick, F. & Mitchison, G. (1983). The function of dream sleep. *Nature*, 304, 111–114.

De Koninck, J., Prevost, F. & Lortie-Lussier, M. (2003). Vertical inversion of the visual field and REM sleep mentation. *Dreaming*, 13, 83–93.

DeCicco, T. L., Donati, D. & Pini, M. (2012). Examining dream content and meaning of dreams with English and Italian versions of the storytelling method of dream interpretation. *International Journal of Dream Research*, 5, 68–75.

Dement, W. (1966). Psychophysiology of Sleep and Dreams. In S. Arieti (eds.), *American Handbook of Psychiatry*. New York: Basic Books.

Deserno, H. (1999). *Das Jahrhundert der Traumdeutung*. Stuttgart: Klett-Cotta.

Deserno, H. & Kächele, H. (2013). Traumserien: Ihre Verwendung in Psychotherapie und Therapieforschung. In B. Janta, B. Unruh & S. Walz-Pawlita (eds.), *Der Traum*. Giessen: Psychosozial.

Desteian, J. A. (1989). *Coming Together – Coming Apart: The Union of Opposites in Love Relationships*. Boston: Sigo Press.

Dieckmann, H. (1965). Integration process of the ego-complex in dreams. *Journal of Analytical Psychology*, 10(1).

Diemer, R. A., Lobell, L. K., Vivino, B. L. & Hill, C. E. (1996). Comparison of dream interpretation, event interpretation and unstructured sessions in brief therapy. *Journal of Consulting Psychology*, 43, 99–112.

Döll-Hentschker, S. (2008). *Die Veränderung von Träumen in psycho-analytischen Behandlungen.* Frankfurt a. M:Brandes & Apsel.

Domhoff, G. W. (1996). *Finding Meaning in Dreams: A Quantitative Approach.* New York: Plenum Press.

Domhoff, G. W. (2003). *The Scientific Study of Dreams: Neural Networks, Cognitive Development, and Content Analysis.* Washington: American Psychological Association.

Domhoff, G. W. & Fox, K. C. (2015). Dreaming and the default network: A review, synthesis, and counterintuitive research proposal. *Consciousness and Cognition,* 33, 342–353.

Domhoff, G. W. & Schneider, A. (2018). Are dreams social simulations? Or are they enactments of conceptions and personal concerns? An empirical and theoretical comparison of two dream theories. *Dreaming,* 28(1), 1–22.

Edwards, C. L., Ruby, P. M., Malinowski, J. E., Bennett, P. D. & Blagrove, M. T. (2013). Dreaming and insight. *Frontiers in Psychology,* 4, 979.

Ellis, L. A. (2016). Qualitative changes in recurrent PTSD nightmares after focusing-oriented dreamwork. *Dreaming,* 26(3), 185–199.

Enke, H., Ohlmeier, D. & Nast, J. (1968). A formal affect and social relation analysis in series of dreams in patients with psychophysiologic disorders. *Zeitschrift für Psychosomatische Medizin und Psychoanalyse,* 14(1), 15–33.

Erikson, E. H. (1955). Das Traummuster der Psychoanalyse. *Psyche,* 8, 561–604.

Ermann, M. (1995). Die Traumerinnerung bei Patienten mit psychogenen Schlafstörungen: Empirische Befunde und einige Folgerungen für das Verständnis des Träumens. In Sigmund Freud Institut (eds.), *Traum und Gedächtnis.* Münster: LIT-Verlag.

Ermann, M. (2005). *Träume und Träumen.* Stuttgart: Kohlhammer.

Eudell-Simmons, E. M. & Hilsenroth, M. J. (2005). A review of empirical research supporting four conceptual uses of dreams in psychotherapy. *Clinical Psychology & Psychotherapy,* 12(4), 255–269.

Euler, J., Henkel, M., Bock, A. & Benecke, C. (2016). Strukturniveau, Abwehr und Merkmale von Träumen. *Forum der Psychoanalyse,* 32, 267–284.

Fairbairn, W. R. D. (1952). *Psychoanalytic Studies of the Personality.* London: Tavistock.

Falk, D. R. & Hill, C. E. (1995). The effectiveness of dream interpretation groups for women undergoing a divorce transition. *Dreaming,* 5, 29–42.

Finke, J., Deloch, H. & Stumm, G. (2019). *Personenzentrierte Psychotherapie und Beratung.* Munich: Reinhardt.

Fischer, C. (1978). *Der Traum in der Psychotherapie: Ein Vergleich Freud'scher u. Jung'scher Patiententräume.* Munich: Minerva.

Fischmann, T. & Leuschner, W. (2008). Kann die psychoanalytische Traumtheorie experimentell gestützt werden? In G. Poscheschnik (eds.), *Empirische Forschung in der Psychoanalyse* (pp. 121–141). Giessen: Psychosozial.

Fischmann, T. & Leuzinger-Bohleber, M. (2018). Traum und Depression. In W. Berner, G. Amelung, A. Boll-Klatt & U. Lamperter (eds.), *Von Irma zu Amalie: Der Traum und seine psychoanalytische Bedeutung im Wandel der Zeit* (pp. 163–182). Giessen: Psychosozial.

Fischmann, T., Leuzinger-Bohleber, M. & Kächele, H. (2012). Traumforschung in der Psychoanalyse: Klinische Studien, Traumserien, extraklinische Forschung im Labor. *Psyche*, 66, 833–861.

Fisher, S. & Greenberg, R. P. (1977). *The Scientific Credibility of Freud's Theories and Therapy.* Hassocks: Harvester Press.

Fisher, S. & Greenberg, R. P. (1996). *Freud Scientifically Reappraised: Testing the Theories and Therapy.* New York: Wiley.

Fiss, H. (1979). Current Dream Research: A Psychobiological Perspective. In B. Wolman (ed.), *A Handbook of Dreams* (pp. 20–75). New York: Van Nostrand.

Fiss, H. (1995). The Post-Freudian Dream: A Reconsideration of Dream Theory based on Recent Sleep Laboratory Findings. In H. Bareuther, K. Brde, M. Evert-Saleh, & N. Spangenberg (eds.), *Traum und Gedächtnis: Materialien aus dem Sigmund-Freud Institut* (pp. 11–35). Münster: LIT.

Fonagy, P., Kächele, H., Leuzinger-Bohleber, M. & Taylor, D. (2012). *The Significance of Dreams: Bridging Clinical and Extraclinical Research in Psychoanalysis.* London: Karnac.

Fosshage, J. L. (1987). New Vistas on Dream Interpretation. In M. Glucksman (ed.), *Dreams in New Perspective: The Royal Road Revisited* (pp. 23–43). New York: Uman Sciences Press.

Fosshage, J. L. (1997). The organizing functions of dreaming mentation. *Contemporary Psychoanalysis*, 33, 429–458.

Foulkes, D. (1982a). How is the Dream Formed? In R. Woods & H. Greenhouse (eds.), *The New World of Dreams* (pp. 303–313). New York: Macmillan.

Foulkes, D. (1982b). You Think All Night Long. In R. Woods & H. Greenhouse (eds.), *The New World of Dreams* (pp. 298–319). New York: Macmillan.

Foulkes, D. (1999). *Children's Dreaming and the Development of Consciousness.* Cambridge: Harvard Universities Press.

French, T. M. (1954). *The Integration of Behavior. Vol. II: The Integrative Process in Dreams.* Chicago: University of Chicago Press.

Freud, S. (1900). *The Interpretation of Dreams.* Standard Edition, IV–V. London: Hogarth.

Freud, S. (1913). *The Claims of Psycho-analysis to Scientific Interest.* SE, 13. London: Hogarth.

Freud, S. (1916/17). *Introductory Lectures on Psycho-Analysis.* SE, 15. London: Hogarth.

Freud, S. (1933). *New Introductory Lectures on Psycho-Analysis.* SE, 22. London: Hogarth.

Gazzillo, F., Silberschatz, G., Fimiani, R., De Luca, E., & Bush, M. (2019). Dreaming and adaptation: The perspective of control-mastery theory. *Psychoanalytic Psychology.* Advance online publication.

Gazzillo, F., Silberschatz, G., Fimiani, R., De Luca, E. & Bush, M. (2020). Dreaming and adaptation: The perspective of control-mastery theory. *Psychoanalytic Psychology*, 37(3), 185–198.

Gendlin, E. T. (1987). *Dein Körper – Dein Traumdeuter.* Salzburg: Müller.

Traumwerkstatt. (1998). *Träume in der Paartherapie.* Göttingen: Vandenhoeck & Ruprecht.

Gennaro, A., Kipp, S., Viol, K., de Felice, G., Andreassi, S., Aichhorn, W. & Schiepek, G. (2020). A phase transition of the unconscious: Automated text analysis of dreams in psychoanalytic psychotherapy. *Frontiers in Psychology*, 11, 1667.

Giovanardi, G. (2021). Working on dreams, from neuroscience to psychotherapy. *Research in Psychotherapy: Psychopathology, Process and Outcome*, 24(2), 230–242.

Glaser, B. G. & Strauss, A. L. (2009). *The Discovery of Grounded Theory: Strategies for Qualitative Research.* New Brunswick: Aldine Transaction.

Glucksman, M. L. & Kramer, M. (2011). The clinical and predictive value of the initial dream of treatment. *Journal of the American Academy of Psychoanalysis and Dynamic Psychiatry*, 39(2), 263–283.

Glucksman, M. L. & Kramer, M. (2015). The Manifest Dream Report and Clinical Change. In M. Kramer & M. Glucksman (eds.), *Dream Research: Contributions to Clinical Practice* (pp. 107–123). London: Routledge.

Greenberg, R. & Pearlman, C. (1978). If Freud only knew: A reconsideration of psychoanalytic dream theory. *International Review of Psycho-Analysis*, 5, 71–75.

Güven, E. & Bilim, G. (2018). An integrative model proposal about underlying mechanisms involved in disturbing dream themes: Defense styles, dysfunctional attitudes, interpersonal styles, and dream themes. *Dreaming*, 28(3), 261–277.

Hall, C. S. (1966). *The Meaning of Dreams*. New York: McGraw-Hill.

Hall, C. S. & Nordby, V. J. (1972). *The Individual and His Dreams*. New York: Signet.

Hall, C. S. & Van De Castle, R. L. (1966). *The Content Analysis of Dreams*. New York: Appleton-Century-Crofts.

Hallschmid, M. & Born, J. (2006). Der Schlaf der Vernunft gebiert Wissen. In M. H. Wiegand, F. von Spreti & H. Förstl (eds.), *Schlaf und Traum: Neurobiologie, Psychologie, Therapie* (pp. 75–106). Stuttgart: Schattauer.

Hamburger, A. (1999). Traum und Sprache. In H. Deserno (eds.), *Das Jahrhundert der Traumdeutung: Perspektiven psychoanalytischer Traumforschung* (pp. 289–327). Stuttgart: Klett-Cotta.

Hamburger, A. (2006). Traum und Zeit – Traumerzählungen als Elemente der Spannungsdramaturgie. *Forum Psychoanalyse*, 22, 23–43.

Hannich, H. J. (2018). *Individualpsychologie nach Alfred Adler*. Stuttgart: Kohlhammer.

Hartmann, E. (1973). *The Functions of Sleep*. New Haven: Yale University Press.

Hartmann, E. (1995). Making connections in a safe place: Is dreaming psychotherapy? *Dreaming*, 5, 213–228.

Hartmann, E. (1996). Outline for a theory on the nature and functions of dreaming. *Dreaming*, 6, 147–170.

Hartmann, E. (1998). *Dreams and Nightmares: The New Theory on the Origin and Meaning of Dreams*. New York: Plenum Trade.

Hartmann, E. (2010). *The Nature and Functions of Dreaming*. New York: Oxford University Press.

Hau, S. (2018). Experimentelle Schlaf- und Traumforschung. In A. Krovoza & C. Walde (eds.), *Traum und Schlaf: Ein interdisziplinäres Handbuch* (pp. 275–286). Stuttgart: J. B. Metzler.

Hill, C. E. (1996). *Working with Dreams in Psychotherapy*. New York: Guildford Press.

Hill, C. E. (2004). *Dream Work in Therapy: Facilitating Exploration, Insight, and Action*. Washington: American Psychological Association.

Hill, C. E., Diemer, R. A. & Heaton, K. J. (1997). Dream interpretation sessions: Who volunteers, who benefits, and what volunteer clients view as most hand least helpful. *Journal of Counselling Psychology*, 44, 53–62.

Hill, C. E., Diemer, R., Hess, S., Hillyer, A. & Seeman, R. (1993). Are the effects of dream interpretation on session quality, insight and emotion due to the dream itself, to projection or to the interpretation process? *Dreaming*, 3, 269–280.

Hill, C. & Knox, S. (2010). The use of dreams in modern psychotherapy. *International Review of Neurobiology*, 92, 291–317.

Hill, C. E., Nakayama, E. Y. & Wonnell, T. L. (1998). The effects of description, association, or combined description/association in exploring dream images. *Dreaming*, 8, 1–13.

Hill, C. E. & Rochlen, A. (2004). The Hill Cognitive-Experiental Model of Dream Interpretation. In R. Rosner, W. Lyddon *et al.* (eds.), *Cognitive Therapy and Dreams* (pp. 161–178). New York: Springer.

Hill, C. E. & Spangler, P. (2007). Dreams and Psychotherapy. In D. Barrett & P. McNamara (eds.). *The New Science of Dreaming. Vol. 2: Content, Recall and Personality Correlates* (pp. 159–186). Wesport: Praeger.

Hobson, A. & McCarley, R. W. (1971). Cortical unity activity in sleeping and waking. *Electroencephalography and Clinical Neurophysiology*, 30, 97–112.

Hobson, A. & McCarley, R. W. (1977). The brain as a dream-state generator: An activation-synthesis-hypothesis of the dream process. *American Journal of Psychiatry*, 134, 1335–1348.

Hobson, J. A. & Schredl, M. (2011). The continuity and discontinuity between waking and dreaming: A dialogue between Michael Schredl and Allan Hobson concerning the adequacy and completeness of these notions. *International Journal of Dream Research*, 4(1), 3–7.

Horton, C. & Malinowski, J. (2015). Autobiographical memory and hyperassociativity in the dreaming brain: Implications for memory consolidation in sleep. *American Journal of Psychiatry*, 134, 1335–1348.

Hoss, R. J. (2011). The continuity and discontinuity between waking and dreaming from the perspective of an analytical psychological construct. *International Journal of Dream Research*, 4(2), 81–83.

Iftikhar, M., Tahir, K., Falak, S. & Shabbir, N. (2020). Dreams and waking life connection. *International Journal of Dream Research*, 220–228.

Jiménez, J. P. (2012). Tradition und Erneuerung in der Traumdeutung. *Psyche: Zeitschrift für Psychoanalyse*, 66(9–10), 803–832.

Jung, C. G. (1944). *Psychologie und Alchemie*. Zurich: Rascher.

Jung, C. G. (1971). *Allgemeine Gesichtspunkte zur Psychologie des Traumes*. GW, Bd. 8. Olten: Walter.

Jung, C. G. (1972). *Traumsymbole des Individuationsprozesses*. GW, Bd. 12. Olten: Walter.

Jung, C. G. (1984). *Die praktische Verwendbarkeit der Traumanalyse*. GW, Bd. 16. Olten: Walter.

Jung, C. G. (2001). *Seminare Kinderträume*. Olten: Walter.

Kächele, H. (2012). Dreams as Subject of Psychoanalytical Treatment Research. In P. Fonagy, H. Kächele, M. Leuzinger-Bohleber & D. Taylor (eds.), *The Significance of Dreams: Bridging Clinical and Extraclinical Research in Psychoanalysis* (pp. 89–100). London: Karnac.

Kächele, H., Eberhardt, J. & Leuzinger-Bohleber, M. (1999). Expressed Relationships, Dream Atmosphere and Problem Solving in Amalia's Dreams—Dream Series as Process Tool to Investigate Cognitive Changes—A Single Case Study. *Psychoanalytic Process Research Strategies II.* Ulm: Ulmer Textbank.

Kächele, H., Leuzinger-Bohleber, M., Buchheim, A. & Thomä, H. (2006). Psychoanalytische Einzelfallforschung: Amalie X – ein Deutscher Musterfall. *Psyche, 60*(5), 387–425.

Kalsched, D. (1996). *The Inner World of Trauma.* London: Routledge.

Kempe, S., Köpp, W. & Wittmann, L. (2024). Personality Functioning Improvement during psychotherapy is associated with an enhanced capacity for affect regulation in dreams: A preliminary study. *Brain Sciences,* 14, 489.

Kirsch, T. (1968). The relationship of the REM state to analytical psychology. *American Journal of Psychiatry,* 124(10), 1459–1463.

Kohut, H. (1977). *The Restoration of the Self.* New York: International Universities Press.

Köthe, M. & Pietrowsky, R. (2001). Behavioral effects of nightmares and their correlation to personality patterns. *Dreaming,* 11, 43–52.

Kramer, M. (1964). Patterns of dreaming: The interrelationship of the dreams of a night. *Journal of Nervous Mental Disease,* 139, 426–439.

Kramer, M. (2015). Establishing the Meaning of a Dream. In M. Kramer & M. Glucksman (eds.), *Dream Research: Contributions to Clinical Practice* (pp. 1–13). London: Routledge.

Kramer, M. & Glucksman, M. (2015). *Dream Research: Contributions to Clinical Practice.* London: Routledge.

Kramer, M., Hlasny, R., Jacobs, G. & Roth, T. (1976). Do dreams have meaning? An empirical inquiry. *American Journal of Psychiatry,* 133, 778–781.

Kramer, M. & Hoffmann, R. (1993). *The Functions of Dreaming.* Albany: State University of New York Press.

Kron, T. & Avny, N. (2003). Psychotherapists' dreams about their patients. *Journal of Analytical Psychology,* 48, 317–339.

Kuiken, D. & Sikora, S. (1993). The Impact of Dreams on Waking Thoughts and Feelings. In A. Moffit, M. Kramer & R. Hoffmann (eds.), *The Functions of Dreaming* (pp. 419–476). Albany: State University of New York Press.

Leuschner, W. (1999). Experimentelle psychoanalytische Traumforschung. In H. Deserno (ed.), *Das Jahrhundert der Traumdeutung* (pp. 356–374). Stuttgart: Klett Cotta.

Leuzinger-Bohleber, M. (1989). *Veränderung kognitiver Prozesse in Psychoanalyse. Bd. II: Fünf aggregierte Einzelfallstudien.* Ulm: PSZ.

Leuzinger-Bohleber, M. (2013). Emodiment – Traum(a) – Depression. In B. Janta, B. Unruh & S. Walz-Pawlita (eds.), *Der Traum.* Giessen: Psychosozial.

Levin, R. (1990). Psychoanalytic Theories on the Function of Dreaming: A Review of the Empirical Dream Research. In J. M. Masling (ed.), *Empirical Studies of Psychoanalytic Theories.* Hillsdale: Erlbaum.

Levy, R., Ablon, S., Ackerman, J., Thomä, H. & Kächele, H. (2012). A Specimen Session of Psychoanalytic Therapy under the Lens of the Psychotherapy Process Q-set. In R. Levy, S. Ablon & H. Kächele (eds.), *Psychodynamic Psychotherapy Research* (pp. 509–528). New York: Humana.

Maggiolini, A., Morelli, M., Falotico, E. & Montali, L. (2016). Dream contents of early adolescents, adolescents, and young adults: A cluster analysis with T-LAB. *Dreaming*, 26 (3), 221–237.

Marcus, E. R. (2003). Medical student dreams about medical school: The unconscious developmental process of becoming a physician. *International Journal of Psychoanalysis*, 84, 367–386.

Mathys, H. (2001). „... ich hab heut Nacht so einen herrlichen Mist geträumt...": Amaliens Traumerzählungen untersucht mit der Erzählanalyse JAKOB. Unpublished thesis. University of Zurich.

McCarley, R. & Hobson, A. (1979). The Form of Dreams and the Biology of Sleep. In B. Wolman (ed.), *A Handbook of Dreams* (pp. 76–130). New York: Van Nostrand.

Mendonça, G. P. D. & Fortim, I. (2018). Study on pediatric oncology patients' dreams. *Jungiana*, 36(2), 55–66.

Mentzos, S. (1995). Traumsequenzen: Zur Psychodynamik der Traumdramaturgie. *Psyche*, 49(7), 653–671.

Mergenthaler, E., Neudert-Dreyer, L., Pokorny, D. & Thomä, H. (2006). The German specimen case Amalia X: Empirical studies. *The International Journal of Psychoanalysis*, 87, 809–826.

Merkle, G. (1987). Veränderungen des Trauminhaltes während einer Psychoanalyse. Dissertation. University of Ulm.

Meltzer, D. (1983). *Dream – Life – A Re-Examination of the Psychoanalytical Theory and Technique.* Strathclyde: Clunie Press.

Mitscherlich, A. (1983). *Gesammelte Schriften: Psychosomatik, Bd. 2.* Frankfurt a. M: Suhrkamp.

Moffitt, A., Kramer, M. & Hoffmann, R. (1993). *The Functions of Dreaming*. Albany: State University of New York Press.

Morgenthaler, C. (1992). *Der religiöse Traum: Erfahrungen und Deutung*. Stuttgart: Kohlhammer.

Morgenthaler, F. (1986). *Der Traum: Fragmente zur Theorie und Technik der Traumdeutung*. Frankfurt a. M.: Campus.

Moser, U. (1999). Selbstmodelle und Selbstaffekte im Traum. *Psyche*, 53, 222–248.

Moser, U. (2003). Traumtheorien und Traumkultur in der psychoanalytischen Praxis. *Psyche*, 57, 639–657.

Moser, U. & von Zeppelin, I. (1991). *Cognitive-Affective Processes*. Berlin: Springer.

Moser, U. & von Zeppelin, I. (1996). *Der geträumte Traum: Wie Träume entstehen und sich verändern*. Stuttgart: Kohlhammer.

Nielsen, T., & Lara-Carrasco, J. (2007). Nightmares, Dreaming, and Emotion Regulation: A Review. In D. Barrett & P. McNamara (eds.), *The New Science of Dreaming, Vol. 2: Content, Recall and Personality Correlates* (pp. 253–284). Westport: Praeger.

Nielsen, T. & Levin, R. (2007). Nightmares: A new neurocognitive model. *Sleep Medicine Review*, 11, 295–310.

Nielsen, T., Zadra, A., Simard, V., Saucier, S., Stenstrom, P., Smith, C. & Kuiken, D. (2003). The typical dreams of Canadian university students. *Dreaming*, 13, 211–235.

OPD-Task Force (eds.) (2008). *Operationalized Psychodynamic Diagnosis OPD-2: Manual of Diagnosis and Treatment Planning*. Göttingen: Hogrefe.

Pagel, J. F. (2015). Positive Aspects of Classic Nightmares. In M. Kramer & M. Glucksman (eds.), *Dream Research: Contributions to Clinical Practice* (pp. 161–173). London: Routledge.

Palombo, S. R. (1982). How the Dream Works: The Role of Dreaming in the Psychotherapeutic Process. In S. Slipp (ed.), *Curative Factors in Dynamic Psychotherapy* (pp. 223–242). New York: McGraw Hill.

Peräkylä, A. & Bergmann, J. (2020). Practices of joint meaning creation: Dreams in psychoanalytic discussion. *The International Journal of Psychoanalysis*, 101(5), 923–950.

Perls, F. S., Hefferline, R. F. & Goodman, P. (2006). *Gestalt-Therapie: Grundlagen der Lebensfreude und Persönlichkeitsentfaltung*. Stuttgart: Klett-Cotta.

Perogamvros, L., Dang-Vu, T. T., Desseiles, M. & Schwartz, S. (2013). Sleep and dreaming are for important matters. *Frontiers in Psychology*, 4, 474.

Pfeifer, L. (2022). Wie Erzählungen Hinweise auf psychische Störungen geben können. *Psychotherapeut*, 67(2), 116–121.

Picchioni, D. & Hicks, R. A. (2009). Differences in the relationship between nightmares and coping with stress for Asians and Caucasians: A brief report. *Dreaming*, 19, 108–112.

Popp, C., Luborsky, L. & Crits-Christoph, P. (1990). The Parallel of the CCRT from Therapy Narratives with the CCRT from Dreams. In L. Luborsky & P. Crits-Christoph, *Understanding Transference: The CCRT Method* (pp. 158–172). New York: Basic Books.

Propp, V. (1975). *Morphologie des Märchens*. Frankfurt a. M.: Surkamp.

Revonsuo, A., Tuominen, J. & Valli, K. (2015). The Avatars in the Machine: Dreaming as a Simulation of Social Reality. In T. Metzinger & J. M. Windt (eds.), *Open MIND* (pp. 1–28). Frankfurt a. M.: MIND Group.

Robbins, P. R. & Tanck, R. H. (1980). Sexual gratification and sexual symbolism in dreams: Some support for Freud's theory. *Bulletin of the Menninger Clinic*, 44, 49–58.

Rodenbeck, A., Gruber-Rüther, A. & Rüther, E. (2006). Affekte im Traum und Wacherleben – eine Affekthypothese des Traumes. In M. H. Wiegand, F. von Spreti & H. Förstl (eds.), *Schlaf und Traum: Neurobiologie, Psychologie, Therapie* (pp. 115–130). Stuttgart: Schattauer.

Roesler, C. (2018a). Structural Dream Analysis: A narrative research method for investigating the meaning of dream series in analytical psychotherapies. *International Journal of Dream Research*, 11(1), 21–29.

Roesler, C. (2018b). Dream content corresponds with dreamer's psychological problems and personality structure and with improvement in psychotherapy: A typology of dream patterns in dream series of patients in analytical psychotherapy. *Dreaming*, 28(4), 303–321.

Roesler, C. (2021). *The Archetype Concept of C. G. Jung – Theory, Research, and Applications*. London: Routledge.

Roesler, C., Kissling, L., Sütterlin, T. & Gees, A. (2024). Dreams in psychotherapy: An empirically supported model of the relations of dreams to the course of psychotherapy. *International Journal of Dream Research*, 17(2), 164–176.

Roesler, C., Konakawa, H. & Tanaka, Y. (2021). Differences in dream content and structure between Japanese and Western dreams. *International Journal of Dream Research*, 14(2), 195–201.

Roth, M. (2003). *Träume in der systemischen Paartherapie*. Göttingen: Vandenhoeck & Rupprecht.

Rüther, E., & Gruber-Rüther, A. (2000). Traum Affekt: Spiel, Theorie, Therapie. *Psyche*, 26, 250–258.

Sándor, P., Szakadát, S. & Bódizs, R. (2016). The development of cognitive and emotional processing as reflected in children's dreams: Active self in an eventful dream signals better neuropsychological skills. *Dreaming*, 26(1), 58–78.

Schredl, M. (2000). The effects of dreams on waking life. *Sleep and Hypnosis*, 2, 120–124.

Schredl, M. (2006). Experimentell-psychologische Traumforschung. In M. H. Wiegand, F. von Spreti & H. Förstl (eds.), *Schlaf und Traum: Neurobiologie, Psychologie, Therapie* (pp. 37–74). Stuttgart: Schattauer.

Schredl, M. (2007). *Träume: Die Wissenschaft enträtselt unser nächtliches Kopfkino*. Berlin: Ullstein.

Schredl, M. (2003). Continuity between waking and dreaming: A proposal for a mathematical model. *Sleep and Hypnosis*, 5, 38–52.

Schredl, M. (2015). The Continuity between Waking and Dreaming: Empirical Research and Clinical Implications. In M. Kramer & M. Glucksman (eds.), *Dream Research: Contributions to Clinical Practice* (pp. 27–37). London: Routledge.

Schredl, M. (2018). *Researching Dreams: The Fundamentals*. Cham: Palgrave Macmillan.

Schredl, M., Germann, L. & Rauthmann, J. (2022). Recurrent dream themes: Frequency, emotional tone, and associated factors. *Dreaming*, 32(3), 235–248.

Solms, M. (2000). Dreaming and REM sleep are controlled by different brain mechanisms. *Behavioral and Brain Sciences*, 23, 843–850.

Solms, M. (2011). Neurobiology and the neurological basis of dreaming. *Handbook of Clinical Neurology*, 98, 519–544.

Solms, M. (2013a). Der Wunsch im Traum – eine neuropsychoanalytische Perspektive. In B. Boothe (ed.), *Wenn doch nur – ach hätte ich bloß: Die Anatomie des Wunsches* (pp. 126–140). Zurich: Rüffer & Rub.

Solms, M. (2013b). Freuds Primärprozeß versus Hobsons Protobewusstsein. In B. Janta, B. Unruh & S. Walz-Pawlita (eds.), *Der Traum*. Giessen: Psychosozial.

Spangler, P. T. & Hill, C. E. (2015). The Hill Cognitive-Experiential Model. In M. Kramer & M. Glucksman (eds.), *Dream Research: Contributions to Clinical Practice* (pp. 123–134). London: Routledge.

Sparrow, G. S. (2020). The construction and analysis of dream metaphors from the standpoint of co-creative dream theory. *Dreaming*, 13(1), 1–9.

Spitzer, M., Walder, S. & Clarenbach, P. (1993). Aktivierte assoziative Netzwerke im REM-Schlaf: Semantische Bahnungseffekte nach dem Aufwecken aus verschiedenen Schlafstadien. In K. Meier-Ewert & E. Rühle (eds.), *Schlafmedizin* (pp. 168–178). Stuttgart: Fischer.

Stevens, A. (1995). *Private Myths: Dreams and Dreaming*. London: Hamish Hamilton.

Stolorow, R. (1978). Themes in dreams: A brief contribution to therapeutique technique. *The International Journal of Psycho-Analysis*, 59, 473–475.

Stolorow, R. & Atwood, G. (1993). Psychoanalytic Phenomenology of the Dream. In S. Flanders (ed.), *The Dream Discourse Today* (pp. 213–228). London: Routledge.

Strauch, I. & Meier, B. (2004). *Den Träumen auf der Spur: Zugang zur modernen Traumforschung*. Bern: Huber.

Varvin, S., Fischmann, T., Jovic, V., Rosenbaum, B., & Hau, S. (2012). Traumatic Dreams: Symbolisation Gone Astray. In P. Fonagy*et al.* (eds.), *The Significance of Dreams* (pp. 182–211). London: Karnac.

Vedfelt, O. (1997). *Dimensionen der Träume*. Düsseldorf: Walter.

Vedfelt, O. (2017). *A Guide to the World of Dreams*. London: Routledge.

Vinocur Fischbein, S. (2011). The use of dreams in the clinical context: Convergencies and divergencies: An interdisciplinary proposal. *International Journal of Psychoanalysis*, 92, 333–358.

Wagner, U., Gais, S., Haider, H., Verleger, R. & Born, J. (2004). Sleep inspires insight. *Nature*, 427, 352–355.

Warner, S. L. (1983). Can psychoanalytic treatment change dreams? *Journal of the American Academy of Psychoanalysis*, 11(2), 299–316.

Weiss, J. (1993). *How Psychotherapy Works: Process and Technique*. New York: Guildford.

Werner, C. & Langenmayr, A. (2005). *Der Traum und die Fehlleistungen: Psychoanalyse und Empirie Bd. 2*. Göttingen: Vandenhoeck & Ruprecht.

Windt, J. M. (2015). *Dreaming*. Cambridge: MIT Press.

Windt, J. M. (2018). Kognitionswissenschaften und Philosophie. In A. Krovoza & C. Walde (eds.), *Traum und Schlaf: Ein interdisziplinäres Handbuch* (pp. 233–247). Stuttgart: J. B. Metzler.

Wright, J. & Koulack, D. (1987). Dreams and contemporary stress: A disruption-avoidance-adaptation model. *Sleep*, 10, 172–179.

Yu, C. K. C. (2013). The structural relations between the superego, instinctual affect, and dreams. *Dreaming*, 23, 145–155.

Zadra, A. & Domhoff, G. W. (2010). Dream Content: Quantitative Findings. In H. M. Kryger, T. Roth & W. C. Dement (eds.), *Principles and Practice of Sleep Medicine* (pp. 585–594). Philadelphia: Saunders/Elsevier.

Index

Note: Page numbers in *italics* indicate figures, and page numbers in **bold** indicate tables in the text

For Product Safety Concerns and Information please contact our EU
representative GPSR@taylorandfrancis.com
Taylor & Francis Verlag GmbH, Kaufingerstraße 24, 80331 München, Germany

www.ingramcontent.com/pod-product-compliance
Lightning Source LLC
Chambersburg PA
CBHW070346270326
41926CB00017B/4016

* 9 7 8 1 0 3 2 7 4 4 2 9 2 *